7 Successful Strategies to Promote Emotional Intelligence in the Classroom

Marziyah Panju

continuum

Continuum International Publishing Group
The Tower Building   80 Maiden Lane, Suite 704
11 York Road   New York, NY 10038
London
SE1 7NX

www.networkcontinuum.co.uk
www.continuumbooks.com

British Library Cataloguing-in-Publication Data
A catalogue record for this book is available from the British Library.

ISBN: 978-1-8553-9439-1

Library of Congress Cataloging-in-Publication Data
Panju, Marziyah.
    7 successful stategies to promote emotional intelligence in the classroom / Marziyah
Panju. – 1st ed.
        p. cm.
    Includes bibliographical references and index.
    ISBN 978-1-85539-439-1
1. Affective education 2. Emotional intelligence. 3. Social learning. 4. Emotions
and cognition. I. Title. II. Title: Seven successful strategies to promote emotional intelligence
in the classroom.

LB1072.P36 2008
370.15'34–dc22   2007044297

Typeset by Aarontype Limited, Easton, Bristol
Printed and bound in Great Britain by MPG Books Ltd

Contents

Introduction

One of the essential requirements of our education system is that it reflects the world around us. Rapid changes are taking place in our society and in our economy, fuelled by the continuous improvement in technology. Consequently, our workplaces are becoming more specialized; teams of people must accomplish their work by collaborating, problem solving and communicating well with each other. One of the most important things schools can do to prepare their learners for life in such a world is to address Emotional Intelligence in the classroom. Teachers can be the most powerful force in modelling and teaching learners how to control anger, respect other people's feelings, resolve conflicts and motivate themselves and others. The ideal learning environment of today must therefore combine 'high tech' and 'soft skills' (people skills as opposed to academic facts). Schools need to attend to the 'whole learner' – and learning must embrace the learner's hearts as well as their minds.

Further, the current political agenda for education has come to realize and acknowledge the importance of 'soft skills' for the greater academic achievement of all our children. The UK government's School's programme for Social and Emotional Aspects of Learning (SEAL) for primary, and more recently in 2007 for secondary schools, highlights their commitment to address the social and emotional skills that underpin effective learning.

My personal interest in understanding the impact of Emotional Intelligence on learners, and its relationship with learning, began as a gut-level feeling that didn't go away. As a former primary-school teacher, I have always been interested in how we learn, as much as what we learn. I had noticed that the inability to manage emotions or communicate effectively often led to unresolved and repetitive conflict among learners, low morale and diminished productivity. I quickly realized that we cannot learn without attending to our emotions. Not only that, but also I do not know of anybody who can learn in the absence of a positive relationship. We learn from the people we care about; and yet we somehow pretend that in school that doesn't matter.

Most of us have grown up assuming that the kind of intellectual learning that goes on in our schools has little or nothing to do with our emotions. With the recent advancements in neuroscience, we now know that the emotional centres of the brain are intricately inter-woven with the neo-cortical areas involved in cognitive learning. When a child who is trying to learn is caught up with distressing emotions, the centres for learning are temporarily hampered. The child's attention becomes pre-occupied with whatever may be the source of the trouble. Because attention is itself a limited capacity, the child has that much lesser ability to hear, to understand or to remember what the teacher or the book is saying. In short, there is a direct link between emotions and learning. As educators, it is therefore our duty to understand the role of Emotional Intelligence in the classroom.

Furthermore, as the test-taking reform movement continues to sweep through our schools, with growing emphasis on academic success and school accountability, the idea of incorporating Emotional Intelligence into the classroom is even more relevant and useful than before. Emotions are more important and powerful to the brain than higher-order thinking skills. The essence of Emotional Intelligence is having our emotions working for us rather than against us. We all know that how we feel about ourselves and others can profoundly affect our ability to concentrate, to remember, to think, and to express ourselves. Without Emotional Intelligence, learners have problems following directions, continually go off task, cannot pay attention, and have difficulty working cooperatively. As such, Emotional Intelligence has the potential to enable schools to get on with the business of teaching and learning.

The field of Emotional Intelligence is at a unique point in its history. The majority of teachers today have neither received training in Emotional Intelligence in their college days, nor were they formally taught these skills when they were in school. Nevertheless, they may have been addressing Emotional Intelligence within their educational practices for many years as part of their individual approach to teaching. On the other hand, some teachers may be using techniques that are contradictory to Emotional Intelligence ideas, for example, providing negative feedback to pupils, using sarcasm, or not modelling effective anger-management techniques themselves.

Teachers face enormous challenges meeting both the academic and emotional needs of their learners in the classroom. During my many years as a classroom practitioner, I have seen how the lack of Emotional Intelligence undermines both the teacher and the learner, and conversely, how the use of Emotional Intelligence leads to enhanced learning for both teachers and learners; the learner develops as a 'whole' person, taking responsibility for their own learning. If learner's feelings influence their readiness and ability to learn, then the teacher should be able to respond to, and positively influence, the feelings of the learners. Consequently, teachers need to develop an understanding of what Emotional Intelligence actually stands for, how it can be developed, and how it can be used effectively in their classrooms.

When Emotional Intelligence is embedded in classrooms, the relationship between learners and teachers is transformed, problem solving becomes commonplace, diversity is respected and valued, and democracy and teamwork flourish. This book is designed for teachers who recognize that being effective in the classroom is about 'inside-out' development, and for those who want a brief tour of this popular concept, together with some practical tools that they can use to begin to develop their learners' Emotional Intelligence.

Although much has been written about the theories of Emotional Intelligence, there is very little that is readily accessible for busy teachers in the classroom who have limited time available to trawl through heavyweight literature. This book aims to change that. I have attempted to make this book informative, yet succinct. It is divided into three parts:

- Part 1 begins by introducing the concept of Emotional Intelligence, tracing its history, highlighting its importance, outlining the aspect of measurement and then discussing issues related to teaching it in the classroom.
- Part 2 provides a framework for understanding Emotional Intelligence competencies and illustrates the ways in which one can begin to develop these capabilities in the classroom setting.

- Part 3 addresses my seven successful strategies which form the acronym ELEVATE, there for teachers to implement in their classroom to promote the Emotional Intelligence of their learners and thus enhance their academic achievement. Although the strategies are based on the fundamental ideas in Emotional Intelligence literature, they have been developed through my own personal philosophy and experience. These strategies are a tried and tested method for successfully embedding Emotional Intelligence in the curriculum and have been compiled with the practicalities of a busy classroom in mind.

Through my mentoring meetings with newly qualified teachers, I have discovered that what teachers really want is some very practical guidelines on how they can apply the skills of Emotional Intelligence in their classrooms. This ultimate ideal was at the forefront of my mind when writing this book. 7 *Successful Strategies to Promote Emotional Intelligence in the Classroom* is therefore an easy to follow, hands-on book for teachers to dip into, in order to develop and use Emotional Intelligence as easily, effectively and efficiently as possible.

I have also included two appendices:

- Appendix 1 details an 'Emotional Intelligence self-check' which is split into two parts: questions and quiz scenarios that you can use to prompt learners to consider their own Emotional Intelligence.
- Appendix 2 is a guide to the key influencers in Emotional Intelligence.

And, finally, I have included lists of organizations and further reading that you might find useful for more information on Emotional Intelligence.

Part 1: What is Emotional Intelligence?

The concept of Emotional Intelligence has received much attention in recent years, and has been heralded as the best investment that we can make for ourselves and our children. It is, however, by no means a twenty-first century fad. Aristotle, one of the most influential of the Ancient Greek philosophers, as far back as 384–322 BC, clearly understood the importance of anger management:

> Anyone can be angry – that is easy. But to be angry with the right person, to the right degree, at the right time, for the right purpose and in the right way – that is not easy.

The idea of Emotional Intelligence is thus not new. What is new, however, is the recognition that the cognitive, emotional and social parts of our brain are deeply interconnected and interdependent – that our feelings dramatically influence our thinking, and our behaviours are inseparable from our emotions. Although the importance of this is increasingly recognized, few people are aware of just how vital Emotional Intelligence is for success in every area of life, and that it is possible to improve an individual's Emotional Intelligence.

What are emotions?

Eric Jensen, member of the Society for Neurosciences and author of several brain-based learning books, defines an emotion as a:

> biologically driven cross-cultural response to an environmental stimulus.

Emotions have also been identified as the human beings' warning system as to what is really going on around them. The study of emotion and its practical importance has interested people for many centuries. In the first century BC Publilius Syrus, a Latin writer of maxims, said:

> Rule your feelings, lest your feelings rule you.

The words 'emotions' and 'feelings' are used interchangeably, although in reality a feeling is the response part of the emotion. Emotions are cross-cultural: the same all over the world; while feelings are a learned response towards the emotion, based on the culture in which we grow up.

Emotions can be multi-faceted and sometimes difficult to pin down. In the last decade or so, scientists have discovered a tremendous amount about the role emotions play in our lives. A major contributing factor for many of the problems in our modern society is the unawareness of the key role played by emotions. So let us examine why emotions are so important.

Why are emotions important?

Our emotions are important because **they contain valuable data**. They are a fundamental part of our daily existence. They were designed through millions of years of evolutionary refinement.

Our bodies talk to us through our emotions and tell us what they need to be healthy and happy. If we don't listen to the messages our bodies are sending, we guarantee our own unhappiness. For example, our emotions can guide us to avoid violent and abusive people. Sadness encourages us to grieve, which in turn helps us to value what we have lost, and appreciate what we have left. Happiness and joy guide us to what is good for our mental and physical health.

Our **emotions also communicate messages to others**. For example, the anger in our faces may say 'STAY AWAY' – and people usually do. On the other hand, when we smile we communicate that it is safe to approach us.

Our **emotions are also impulses that compel us towards** – or away from – various courses of action. Without emotions we would not last long: emotions urge us to take action when necessary. The most well-known reaction is the 'fight' or 'flight' principle which causes us to react swiftly to danger by retaliating or running away.

Emotions also enhance our thinking. If we are in a positive mood, we can generate new and interesting ideas. If we are worried or distressed about an issue, then creativity does not flow and we get stuck. Our emotions are a critical ingredient for optimum information processing. When a learner's emotions are engaged, the brain codes the content, and the experience is marked as important and meaningful. Attending consistently and patiently to children's emotions and their consequences as a central part of classroom processes leads to improved personal and academic outcomes. Therefore, healthy strategies for coping with, communicating about, and managing emotions assists children in maintaining attention and focus during academic and inter-personal learning contexts.

Understanding our emotions provides us with information about how we and others tick. The key is to listen to, and use, our emotions intelligently; but how many times have we been culturally taught to deny our basic emotions? For example, girls are encouraged to be 'nice' and 'not angry', while boys are encouraged to be 'strong' and 'not weep'. Such denial can lead to blocks to emotional, and therefore cognitive, development. Fortunately, our society is gradually becoming more comfortable with the idea that emotions are important. We must remember that focusing on our emotions does not make us weak or vulnerable. Instead, it allows us to cope with conflict and change in a constructive manner.

What is Emotional Intelligence?

Like cognitive intelligence, Emotional Intelligence is difficult to define and therefore its definition really depends on whom you ask. There are a number of accepted variations:

Mayer and Salovey, who coined the term Emotional Intelligence, defined it as:

> A learned ability to monitor one's own and other's feelings and emotions, to discriminate among them and to use this information to guide one's thinking and actions. (1997)

Reuvan BarOn, a pioneer in the field of Emotional Intelligence, defined it as:

> An array of non-cognitive capabilities, competencies and skills that influence one's ability to succeed in coping with environmental demands and pressures.

Emotional Intelligence is also the ability to recognize, understand and manage emotions in ourselves and others. Emotional information is all around us. Emotions communicate basic feeling states from one individual to another; they signal urgent messages such as 'let's get together' or 'I am hurting' or 'I'm going to hurt you'. Emotional Intelligence, then, is the ability to use your emotions to help you solve problems and live a more effective life. We can say that Emotional Intelligence is:

> Knowing what feels good, what feels bad, and how to get from bad to good.

Another definition is from Daniel Goleman (1996), an internationally renowned author of the best-seller *Emotional Intelligence* who says that:

> Emotional Intelligence is all about how you handle yourself, get along with people, and work in teams. It is the ability to motivate oneself, and persist in the face of frustration; to control impulse and delay gratification; to regulate one's moods and to empathise with others.

Put very simply, Emotional Intelligence is the ability to be aware of and manage emotions that affect us and others. It is a different way of being smart; it includes ways not measured by IQ. It helps to be aware of our feelings because we can then use them to make good decisions in life. This is critical to the success of all kinds of interactions at home and at school. Emotional Intelligence matters because it enables us to achieve our best and to make a greater contribution to society.

Why is Emotional Intelligence suddenly popular now?

The current popularity of Emotional Intelligence is a reflection of the shift in social attitudes generally, as well as in education. Previously, it was thought that having reasoned arguments between intelligent people was the best way to get to the truth; now, objectivity alone has lost its appeal. Emotions are now the constant counterpart of reason. Emotions originate in the brain just as reason does, even though we might feel them in our heart or in our gut. They are equally valid when making decisions; the key to making informed decisions is to consult both sides of our brain.

Furthermore, in education, teachers too have realized that the traditional curriculum is insufficient to equip young learners to face the realities of the world. They have come to understand the importance of emotions and the role they can play in education, and in our lives generally.

How does Emotional Intelligence differ from Emotional Literacy?

The terms Emotional Intelligence and Emotional Literacy mean more or less the same thing, or at least overlap considerably. The term 'Emotional Intelligence' was popularized by Goleman (1996) and refers to the capacity to acquire and apply information of an emotional nature, to feel and to respond emotionally. It is most commonly used in the United States and in business contexts.

'Emotional Literacy' on the other hand, is used to describe the relative ability to experience and productively manage emotions. It is most commonly used in the UK and in educational contexts. The downside of using the term Emotional Literacy, from a personal perspective, is that it can have negative connotations for those who have disliked the concept of 'the literacy hour' and fear the onset of the 'emotional literacy hour'.

Antidote, a UK organization that campaigns for Emotional Literacy, defines it as

> The practice of thinking individually and collectively about how our emotions shape our actions, and of using emotional understanding to enrich our thinking. (Antidote 2003)

The National Emotional Literacy Interest Group (www.nelig.com) says of Emotional Literacy:

> We all have varying degrees of emotional literacy. The degree to which we are emotionally literate, therefore, reflects the degree to which we are able to recognise, understand, handle and appropriately express our emotions.

How did Emotional Intelligence evolve?

Emotional Intelligence evolved along with humankind. It is as old as time. It is not a fad or a trend, nor is it as new as many people believe. It seems novel only because it was shuffled aside by the twentieth-century fixation on scientific data and rationalism at any cost. The social sciences are only now catching up and becoming acceptable. To gain a practical perspective, let's focus on the development of the concept of Emotional Intelligence in the twentieth century.

Back in 1920, the American psychologist Edward Thorndike talked about something he called 'social intelligence'. Later, the importance of 'emotional factors' was recognized by David Wechsler, one of the fathers of IQ testing. In 1940, in a rarely cited paper, Wechsler urged that the 'non-intellective aspects of human intelligence' be included in any 'complete' measurement. This paper also discussed what he called 'affective' abilities, basically Emotional Intelligence, which he thought would prove critical to an overall view. Unfortunately, this was not included in Wechsler's IQ tests and little attention was paid to it at the time.

Then, in 1948, another American researcher, R. W. Leeper, promoted the idea of 'emotional thought', which he believed contributed to 'logical thought'. But few psychologists or educators pursued this line of questioning until more than 30 years later. In 1983 Howard Gardner, at Harvard University, wrote about the possibility of 'multiple intelligences' including interpersonal and intrapersonal intelligence. He defined 'interpersonal intelligence' as the 'ability to understand people, what motivates them, how they work, and how to work cooperatively with them'; 'intrapersonal intelligence' involved 'access to one's own feelings' and 'the capacity to understand oneself and to use that understanding to operate effectively in their life'.

One of the most significant breakthroughs in Emotional Intelligence took place in 1980, when the American-born Israeli psychologist Dr Reuvan BarOn began his work in the field. He was perplexed by a number of basic questions. Why, he wondered, do some people possess greater emotional well-being? Why are they better able to achieve success in life? And, most importantly, why do some people who are blessed with superior intellectual abilities seem to fail in life, while others with more moderate gifts succeed? By 1985, he thought he had found a partial answer in what he called a person's emotional quotient (EQ), an obvious parallel to the long-standing measures of cognitive or rational abilities that we know as IQ.

Jack Mayer and Peter Salovey coined the term 'Emotional Intelligence' in 1990, and Howard Gardner, the psychologist, used it in his work on 'multiple intelligences', but it was Daniel Goleman, a psychology journalist, who popularized the concept in his 1996 bestselling book of the same name. He brought together the existing body of Emotional Intelligence research with an introduction to how emotion works on the brain, and therefore how to cultivate it in schools and workplaces. He cherry-picked parts that he liked from Gardner's and Mayer and Salovey's understanding and definition of Emotional Intelligence.

What is the history of Cognitive Intelligence (IQ)?

During the past hundred years, cognitive intelligence and the means by which it is measured – that is IQ and IQ testing – have dominated society's views of human potential.

In 1905, the French Psychologist Alfred Binet, together with his colleague the psychiatrist Théodore Simon, developed the first formal intelligence test. Binet had been asked by the Parisian School Commission to come up with a way that children could be categorized according to ability. The aim was actually to weed out the 'feeble-minded', those who would not benefit from a publicly funded system. Binet had long believed that intelligence was an interlocking process that involved judgement, problem solving and reasoning. He and Simon completed and published an IQ test – administered, at first, to children – that enabled him to obtain performance standards for different age groups. These formed the

11

basis of what became known as 'mental ages'. The results would give the mental age of a person in relation to average levels of growth and intellectual development.

In 1910 Binet-Simon tests migrated to the United States where the educator and psychologist Henry Goddard had founded his own school for the 'feeble-minded' in New Jersey. Later the test was modified and standardized for a wider American population by Lewis Terman at Stanford University, and was administered to both children and adults; it became known as Stanford-Binet Test.

The ability to measure cognitive intelligence assumed new importance. Not only could it identify and side-track 'feeble-minded individuals', it could pick out those who scored highly and could be expected to put their learning to best effect. IQ took on a life of its own. It was generally agreed to be a major factor not only in school, but also in the workplace and in personal relationships. But, soon, cracks began to appear, and IQ came under attack.

First there came a number of lengthy debates centring on the influence of genetics and environment: 'nature versus nurture'. Then, stormy controversies arose over cultural and racial differences. By 1960, more and more studies had begun to question the relative importance of cognitive and analytic factors as a measure of overall intelligence. But, given the absence of a solid alternative framework, IQ persisted as the norm, no matter how muddled the original concept had become with the passage of time.

How do IQ and EQ compare with each other?

EQ is not the opposite of IQ. Some people are blessed with a lot of both and some with little of either. What we are trying to establish is how they complement each other. For example, how we handle stress affects our ability to concentrate and put intelligence to use.

Cognitive intelligence refers to the ability to concentrate and plan, to organize material, to use words and to understand, assimilate and interpret facts. In short, IQ is a measure of an individual's personal information bank – one's memory, vocabulary and visual-motor coordination. Emotional Intelligence is the set of socio-emotional skills that enable the intellect to turn into action and accomplishment. Nurturing our Emotional Intelligence creates not only higher achievement in individuals, but also increased on-task behaviours and reduction in discipline problems. Without EQ, IQ remains a potential.

IQ which is strategic (long-term capacity) does not, and cannot, predict success in life, while EQ which is tactical (immediate functioning) can, because it reflects how a person applies his/her knowledge to the immediate situations. Research has shown that when millionaires were asked to rate a list of 30 given factors in order of how important they were in their success, the top five were:

1. Being honest with all people
2. Being well-disciplined
3. Getting along with people
4. Having a supportive spouse
5. Working harder than most people.

All these are reflections of our Emotional Intelligence. In a way, a measure of one's Emotional Intelligence is a measure of one's 'common sense' and the ability to get on in the world.

Can Emotional Intelligence be measured?

Measures of Emotional Intelligence are available to help us better understand our emotional strengths and weaknesses. It can, however, be quite difficult and expensive to measure it accurately.

The easiest and most common way to measure Emotional Intelligence is through the use of what I call 'self-report measures'. Self-report tests have been around for decades and they serve a very useful purpose. They ask the individual to report on his or her own abilities, skills and behaviour; for example, such scales would ask how effective the individual is in recognizing, understanding and controlling their emotions. These tests rely on the fact that individuals can be accurate reporters of their own skills and abilities.

This method is probably the weakest way of measuring Emotional Intelligence because:
- individuals quite often tend to inflate their own strengths and minimize their shortcomings to enhance their self-image;
- even if individuals are completely honest in their own self-reports, they frequently lack accurate insight to appreciate their true character.

People not only colour the truth in their answers, but also in many cases may not even know the truth to start with. Does this mean that self-report measures of Emotional Intelligence should not be used? Well, if we are trying to measure Emotional Intelligence as a set of abilities or skills, then self-report may not be the best method to use. On the other hand, if individuals are interested in identifying their own perception of their emotional strengths and weaknesses, then this may be the preferred approach. For a more objective analysis, we need to consider the alternatives.

Since Emotional Intelligence is all about 'people skills', we can also ask other people what they think of the individuals they associate with. On the face of it, this seems to be a legitimate means of testing Emotional Intelligence, and could even complement the 'self-test measures'. But let's take a closer look at this method, often called Observer Ratings and, in human-resource circles, 360-Degree Assessment.

In this approach, questions about an individual's behaviour are answered not by them, but by people who know them well, such as family, friends or co-workers. The advantages of such observer-rating questionnaires are two-fold:

- firstly, other people are less prone to colour their answers than the individual themselves; and
- secondly, other people are often in a better position to witness and accurately evaluate how skilful the individual is in social interactions.

However, such ratings of behavior are based upon others' observations, as well as their own biases. Some observers may have an axe to grind, and give us uniformly low ratings. Or, if the observers work for us, they may not tell us, even anonymously, that they think our relationship-handling style is atrocious. We must therefore, continue our search for another method.

How do you determine whether you are skilled or not skilled in a particular area? The obvious answer is to directly test the skills in question. If one wants to know if they can type, they take a typing test. A typing test does not ask one how fast they type, nor does it ask a friend how fast they can type. It requires one to type. The approach, therefore, is to use performance tests to measure Emotional Intelligence. These tests present the individuals with practical problems or scenarios and ask them to figure out the correct responses. Instead of asking one to report on how good their Emotional Intelligence skills are, the tests ask them to demonstrate those skills. These tests are less vulnerable to the problems facing self-report and observer-rating tasks, but they are much more difficult to construct, and therefore enormously expensive for individuals.

The most widely used and respected measures of Emotional Intelligence currently available are commercial instruments, afforded only by large organizations. They consist of a blend of self-report measures, observer-rating tests and the performance component. These commercial instruments are typically the result of years of development – of testing, refinement and validation – and so are far too costly to be within the reach of individuals.

Thus, the simple answer is that, if we wish to be aware of our Emotional Intelligence, we can use the self-report measures and/or the observer-ratings test; but, if we wish to measure our abilities to handle emotional situations, then we must indulge in the expensive performance tests.

Why is teaching about Emotional Intelligence more important in the classroom today?

The first point of call for teaching Emotional Intelligence is undoubtedly the home. How parents treat their children has deep and lasting consequences for their emotional life. In order to help children deal constructively with their emotions, parents themselves must have a reasonable degree of Emotional Intelligence. They need to guide their children in handling anger, resolving conflict positively, in impulse control and empathy for others. The children of emotionally competent parents can handle their own emotions and can show empathy to the feelings of others and are better liked by their peers. Parents who show a lack of respect for their child's feelings, or who accept any emotional response as inappropriate, are putting their child at risk when they start school.

In the Western world today, the majority of families have shrunk from an extended community to its bare minimum (one or two parents with one or two children). What is even more revealing is that parents themselves are not always in a position to cope with, or dispense, such emotional skills themselves. Scientific research, in particular on how the brain works, indicates that the establishment of emotional skills is much easier in the 'formative' years from birth to late teens.

Looking at existing societal structures, after the home, the next place most youngsters spend their time is at school. It is therefore left to schools as the place communities can turn to for correctives to children's deficiencies in Emotional Intelligence. Since virtually every child goes to school, it offers a place to teach children the basic lessons for living that they may never get elsewhere.

Children often come to school lacking the capacity to handle their upsets, to listen or focus, or to feel responsible for their work and care about learning. Schools that do not address Emotional Intelligence find it challenging to handle such intake, and a handful of children then end up being excluded from mainstream schooling. Emotional Intelligence can enhance the school's ability to teach, and thus even at a time of back to basics and budget cuts, there is an argument to be made in favour of including Emotional Intelligence in the curriculum. Such programmes help to reverse the tide of educational decline and strengthen schools in accomplishing their main mission, and so are well worth the investment.

Furthermore, we often hear that 'to teach is to touch the heart'. Teachers therefore, have a moral responsibility to enhance pupils' Emotional Intelligence in order to equip them with the tools that will stand by them in the world of work and in their personal life. We now know enough from the research, and also from what employees tell us, to realize that we need the people skills, the team-building skills, the communication skills, and the emotional management skills as much as we need all of those other, more intellectual capacities. So a balance between the academic and the 'soft' skills addresses the whole range of skills that young people will need to equip them to be successful in their personal lives and in their careers.

What is the impact of Emotional Intelligence?

At school, literacy and numeracy are highly valued and need to be at the heart of the curriculum to raise standards, but I believe that they should be equal partners with the promotion of Emotional Intelligence. Emotions have an impact on every area of our lives: academic learning, improvement in behaviour, health and relationships.

Academic learning

Learning is emotion-based. Look at underachieving pupils and you will notice the absence or underdevelopment of an aspect of their Emotional Intelligence. Children with low levels of Emotional Intelligence quickly get bored, or over-anxious, and then look for success and attention elsewhere. Studies have shown that competence in emotional skills results not only in higher academic achievement for the learners, but also in significantly more instructional time for the teachers. This is because emotionally competent learners are far less disruptive and require fewer disciplinary interventions.

Furthermore, academic intelligence, as measured by IQ and SAT scores, is not a reliable predictor of who will succeed in life. Goleman argues that Emotional Intelligence is of much greater importance than academic intelligence in developing a well-rounded person. He stresses that:

> At best, IQ contributes about 20 per cent to the factors that determine life success, which leaves 80 per cent to other forces. (1996)

Numerous studies have shown that IQ has minimal impact on how individuals lead their lives – how happy they are or how successful. One explanation could be that cognitive skills are tied to IQ, but desire and motivation are products of Emotional Intelligence. Your personal ambition can take you that extra mile to achieve your goal. Youngsters with increased emotional competence have an increased desire to learn and to achieve, both within school and outside.

Improvement in behaviour (leading to inclusion)

Teachers who once dealt with mischievous, unruly learners and an occasional temper tantrum now have to deal with violence and disorder to crisis proportions. Emotional Intelligence is one of the tools that can help make inclusion of difficult learners a smoother process. For example, Southampton City Local Authority, which is among those leading the field in developing this work in the UK, set a target of no exclusions for its schools. Since embedding emotional literacy in its schools, exclusions have reduced steadily, year by year, from 113 in 1997 to 22 in 2000. (More up-to-date figures have not yet been published.)

Health

There is no doubt that emotions can profoundly affect our health. The brain, the nervous system and the immune system are all interconnected. Research has shown that those who hide their feelings or refuse to talk about significant emotional crises in their lives are at a higher risk for a variety of health problems. Bottling up our anger and other negative emotions can have toxic effects to our bodies. Numerous studies have also shown that positive, supportive relationships can be good or even better medicine for speeding recovery time or prolonging life.

Relationships

Children who are effective in social interactions are capable of understanding their peers. They are empathetic to their classmates and are effective at being heard and getting help when they need it. Socially competent children can process the verbal and non-verbal messages of others, and recognize that the behaviours of one person can affect another.

Children who cannot interpret or express emotions feel frustrated. They do not understand what is going on around them. They may be viewed as strange. Such children may misinterpret a look or statement and respond inappropriately. Simultaneously, they lack the ability to express their uncertainty or clarify the intentions of others. They may be short of empathy and be totally unaware of how their behaviour affects others.

Can we teach Emotional Intelligence?

The good news is that Emotional Intelligence can be nurtured, developed and augmented. It is not a trait that we either have or don't have. We can increase our Emotional Intelligence at any time in our life as we learn and practise the skills that make up the concept of Emotional Intelligence.

Successful schools include Emotional Intelligence in their curriculum because evidence shows that it is possible to influence learner's Emotional Intelligence skills. People can be taught to become more Emotionally Intelligent, which enables them to become more successful in life. Teachers can instil in learners the ability to be emotionally self-aware, insightful regarding the motivation of others, more able to cope with emotional dilemmas in life, and more empathetic towards their peers. They would also be more socially adept and able to solve problems effectively, resolve conflicts and excel in teamwork activities.

The two most important lessons in the teaching and learning of Emotional Intelligence are:

- Emotions, and how we respond to them, are learned: We learn these from our personal experiences with parents, siblings, friends, teachers and mentors. We are simultaneously influenced by books, films, television, political leaders, sport heroes and other role models. We learn beneficial as well as ineffective or even harmful ways of responding emotionally. Most of this learning is without any deliberate effort on our part but the essence is that we have the capacity to seek out and acquire improved and constructive ways of responding to life situations.
- We can learn to control how we feel and how we respond: Although emotional situations can be very powerful, we can control how we feel and respond to them. Once aware of our emotions, we can make choices as to how to respond so that situations affect us most positively. These skills can be learnt, and then they are in our control.

In light of these two important lessons, the following ideas are some of the generic experiences that teachers can use to develop Emotional Intelligence in the classroom:

- Circle Time, in which learners are able to share emotionally charged issues that concern them and are coached in positive ways of listening and responding to each other (for more on Circle Time, see pp. 67–8)
- Explicit lessons on social, emotional and behavioural skills through role playing real-life situations and problem-solving scenarios
- Modelling constructive relationships
- Use of multiple intelligence to celebrate success of all kinds
- Use Philosophy for Children (P4C) and, through the stories read and discussed, pupils can talk about their feelings, the feelings of others and simultaneously question the rights and wrongs of issues at their level of understanding

- Activate learners' thinking skills
- Active listening to learners' views about their learning experiences
- Training some young people in 'conflict management' which they then make use of in dealing with playground disputes
- Setting quizzes that encourage emotional reflection, empathy and self-awareness
- Teaching explicit techniques such as 'calming down', which enable pupils to stop and think in the heat of the moment and so avoid inflaming situations.

What role do teachers play in teaching Emotional Intelligence?

Emotional Intelligence education probably depends at least as much on the way teachers publicly respond to their own shifting moods and stresses, and the way they deal with the learners in the classroom, as it does on set-piece discussions or activities.

Teachers are crucial role models for learners in this domain. Teachers teach Emotional Intelligence by their being, by how they handle difficult situations such as when some children are having a fight, by how they notice that one child is left out and make sure that they are included, and by how they tune into the social dynamics between the learners' lives. Teachers can use the appropriate vocabulary to discuss emotions and why we feel the way we do and encourage, through example, how to handle positively differences between us. Huge lessons are taught in subtle ways!

What are the teachers' concerns for teaching Emotional Intelligence?

The main concerns held by the teachers are that:
- there is not enough time in the curriculum-packed day
- teachers are accountable for SATs and not Emotional Intelligence
- this is the work of counsellors, social workers and school psychologists
- it is the parents' responsibility and they should be doing it, not us
- this has not been part of our training, and we are not qualified to teach it.

There is not enough time in the curriculum-packed day

The first point to raise here is that Emotional Intelligence is not necessarily an add-on to the existing curriculum. It is something teachers can practise within normal classroom teaching, as well as at other times in the school day such as playtimes and dinner times. The second point is that Emotional Intelligence makes time available for teaching and learning because it enables learners to take on more responsibility for their learning. They are likely to be working more effectively together and finding ways to stimulate each other.

Teachers are accountable for SATs and not Emotional Intelligence

Those responsible for drafting the National Curriculum were explicit about the importance of promoting 'learner's self-esteem and emotional well-being'. They viewed personal development as underpinning academic achievement. Moreover, Emotional Intelligence can lead to richer experiences in learning and enhance academic achievement. The education agenda is increasingly focused on the importance of teaching our youngsters these soft skills so that they might be successful at school and in the workplace.

This is the work of counsellors, social workers and school psychologists

Critics who argue this might have a very short-sighted perspective that ignores the connection between school success and emotional well-being. Academic performance improves when learners are relieved of the stresses that disturb their academic focus. All learners need help to learn and to grow by being given time to think about the feelings they are experiencing in the classroom. Learning and emotions are inextricably linked, and as teachers we need to make it normal practice to address the emotional dynamics at work in the classroom so that we can enhance the learning of all our learners and enable them to reach their true potential.

It is the parents' responsibility and they should be doing it, not us

It is no doubt the responsibility of parents to address Emotional Intelligence of their children in the home. But are they doing so? Learners deserve another chance if their home cannot provide for their emotional well-being. Emotional Intelligence can also be considered as part of a classroom-management strategy. When you build a community of learners, you need to teach the learners about themselves, and about the kind of people they want to be. Then you have fewer management problems, and you can concentrate on the business of teaching the curriculum.

This has not been part of our training, and we are not qualified to teach it

Teachers need adequate training to develop their own Emotional Intelligence before they can be expected to deliver these skills to their pupils. This book is partly in response to that plea!

Summary

A major contributing factor for many of the problems in our society today can be traced to the lack of awareness of the key role played by emotions. Our ability to feel is as vital to our wel-being as our ability to think. Emotional Intelligence can be a positive, preventive tool, which when properly understood can assist our society in solving many of its ills. For it is that set of skills that enables us to use our emotions effectively to liberate the human potential.

The need to engage our learners with the skills of Emotional Intelligence is not only for their period in education, but also increases as they take on higher level of responsibilities such as management of the workforce and parenthood.

What we have learnt from Part 1 is that it is possible to teach Emotional Intelligence in schools. The only stumbling block identified is the need for adequate training for teachers. Nurturing the Emotional Intelligence of teachers is the key to the successful implementation of Emotional Intelligence in schools. Many teachers want to help young people find and deepen a sense of community and purpose, but they cannot give them what they do not have. Therefore, Part 2 directly addresses the issue of supporting teachers in their role as classroom practitioners of Emotional Intelligence.

Emotional Intelligence holds the key to an effective strategy for enabling teachers to promote learning and well-being.

Part 2: Emotional Intelligence Competencies

The basic ingredients of Emotional Intelligence, according to Daniel Goleman are:

- Self-awareness
- Self-control
- Empathy
- Personal motivation
- Relationship skills.

These could also be viewed as a summation of Intrapersonal and Interpersonal Intelligence from Howard Gardner's idea of 'Multiple Intelligences'.

Intrapersonal Intelligence	Interpersonal Intelligence
• Internal intelligences used to understand and motivate ourselves • Self-awareness • Self-control • Personal motivation	• External intelligences used to read, understand and manage our relationship with others • Expressing empathy • Relationship skills

Competencies are behaviours. Behaviours can be taught, practised and ultimately developed. Yet, having a list of competencies makes it appear that they exist all together at one level. The reality is that they are all fundamentally developmental over time. We start by being capable of only a basic performance of some competencies, and then develop more complex levels of attainment as we grow

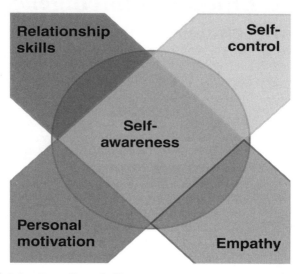

Figure 2.1 Centrality of self-awareness

and mature. In the case of some competencies, such as empathy, the ability even to begin to connect with and understand the feeling of others cannot start until around school-entry age.

Self-awareness is the foundation upon which all other Emotional Intelligence skills are built. It is also the threshold skill, the one that when increased ensures that the other competencies will grow.

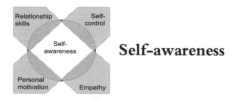

Self-awareness

Self-awareness is the cornerstone of Emotional Intelligence. It is the ability to know our internal states, preferences, resources and intuitions. This would include:

- an emotional awareness: recognizing our emotions as they occur in real life; understanding the causes of these emotions, i.e. what are our triggers?
- accurate self-assessment: knowing our strengths and limits
- self-confidence: a strong sense of our own self-worth and capabilities.

24

In a state of low self-awareness, we act out our feelings without an awareness of their existence. As we develop our sense of self-awareness, we begin to recognize the basic feelings within us. Finally, in a state of high self-awareness, we can differentiate between many emotions. High self-awareness enables us to monitor and observe ourselves in action and influence our actions so that they work to our benefit. For example, when we are aware that our voice is getting louder and we are becoming increasingly angry at a learner who is making yet another reasonable demand, and appreciating our need to stay calm as a model for all our learners, we lower our voice automatically, diffuse our anger and respond respectfully. Had we not recognized that we were getting angry, maybe the situation could have been blown out of control.

What are the skills involved in self-awareness?
- Recognizing our own emotions
- Understanding the causes and impact of our own feelings and actions on us and on others
- Recognizing our strengths
- Being responsible
- Building on our self-image.

Recognizing our own emotions
Our feelings tell us what we really care about, and so there's no right or wrong. We must be able to identify and label our feelings. We need to develop a rich vocabulary of feeling words so as to understand our experiences. Denying our feelings leads to confusion, resentment and physical stress. Even intense and uncomfortable feelings are softened when they are acknowledged without criticism or blame.

Understanding the causes and impact of our feelings and actions on us and on others
Through careful observation we learn what impact our feelings and actions have on others. This knowledge helps us become more effective in our interaction with others. If we feel afraid, what do we need to do to feel safe? Could we decrease our worry by planning ahead a little better next time? Do we need to talk positively to ourselves to get through a stressful time?

Recognizing our strengths
Certainly, we all recognize that there are basically two steps to improving performance. First, we must recognize our weaknesses as well as our strengths. Second, we must enhance our strengths while reducing our weaknesses.

Being responsible
Choosing safe options and being responsible – understanding our obligation to engage in safe behaviours.

Building on our self-image
Self-image is how we perceive ourselves. It is important because how we feel and think about our self affects the way we act. If we disliked some aspect of our self it is important to do something about it.

Why is it important to be self-aware?
Our emotions often interact with each other. The result is a complex emotional world. If we are unaware of, or don't understand our internal state, we can be engulfed in emotions and lose control, with detrimental or even disastrous effects. Goleman describes this feeling of being 'flooded' or overwhelmed by feelings as an *emotional hijacking* and clearly the less self-aware we are the more likely we are to be 'hijacked'.

Furthermore, the capacity to know what we are feeling and how we are behaving allows us a degree of control over our own behaviour. Once an emotional response comes into awareness, the chances of handling it appropriately improves. It is important at all times to be aware of the relationship between our thoughts, our feelings and our actions. What thought sparked off that feeling? What feeling was behind that action? Analysing this sequence can increase our chances for recognizing our impromptu actions, and therefore enable us to stop and think of appropriate responses.

Further, we must be able to identify our own emotions before we can begin to deal effectively with others. Recognizing our own emotions can give us a better insight into what we like, dislike or are ambivalent about; provide us with information about our judgements (e.g. we like something because it made us feel a certain way); give us clues on how to behave; and help us to understand the consequences of our own emotions.

How do we develop self-awareness in the classroom?

- Investigate self-image
- Expand emotional vocabulary
- Validate feelings through open discussion
- Determine the causes and effects of their emotion
- Model self-awareness
- Track emotions for older learners

Investigate self-image

'Who am I?' activities help learners build a positive self-image by helping them to focus on themselves. Get the learners to create a mind-map of their strengths, limitations, roles, responsibilities, qualities, experience and talents.

Ask each learner to choose a person they admire, maybe in a curriculum-related area. Ask them to compare and contrast themselves with this person and create a Venn diagram to show ways they are similar to and different from their chosen hero or heroine. Remember to consider appearance, abilities, interests, intelligence strengths, work ethics and emotional strengths.

Expand emotional vocabulary

- Brainstorm a list of feelings and encourage preciseness to enhance the quality of the list:

Happiness	Anger	Sadness
Excited	Fury	Grief
Joyful	Rage	Sorrow
Cheerful	Resentment	Misery
Glad	Wrath	Pain
Content	Bitterness	Despair
Jovial	Temper	Unhappiness

- Encourage the learners to mime a feeling and get others to guess it.
- Have a collection of different faces from magazines and play 'guess my feelings?'
- At Circle Time, think about a time when they experienced one of those feelings and share it with the group.

- Write a story or a piece of creative writing that uses some of the feeling words.
- Create a painting or drawing to depict an emotion and put up a 'feelings wall' in the classroom or school corridor.
- Encourage the learners to collect newspaper or magazine cuttings of articles or photos that show strong feelings, and make a montage and put it on display.
- Brainstorm all feeling words and attempt as a class or in groups to sort them, identifying their own criteria and negotiating entry into sets.

Validate feelings through open discussion
- Allow an opportunity each day for the learners to share their highs/lows around school and home. This will inform the teacher and their peers about their feelings and in return enable them to validate these feelings.
- Request that the learners bring in a special object and describe their feelings associated with it and explain why.
- Motivate the learners to write a list of feeling words to describe what they like about a friend or relative (a good activity before Mother's/Father's Day) to support poetry writing in the form of an acrostic.

Determine the causes and effects of their emotion
- Discuss with the learners the connection between what they felt, thought and did.
- Identify emotions as they are experienced: What emotion are they experiencing? Why is it there? What does it make them want to do?
- When sharing stories, encourage learners to make the link between the characters' thoughts, feelings and actions. Identify any patterns they observe.

Model self-awareness
- Let your learners know when you are experiencing a strong emotion to which they may be able to relate. Explain your thoughts, feelings and actions. Take a few minutes to let them share a time when they felt the same way.

Track emotions for older learners

Tracking self-awareness: If learners are not sure of how self-aware they are, then they can monitor their self-awareness by keeping a diary for a while and doing a feelings check throughout the day. Label the feeling and rate it on a 10-point scale where 1 = weak or vague and 10 = very powerful.

Having kept the feelings diary, invite them to write a short account of how their mood or feeling changed from one session to another. Can they describe what influenced that change, was the feeling changed deliberately, was the change welcome?

Further, ask them to describe the impact of their feeling(s) on other people, based on their experience described in the diary. For example, if they felt happy, did that help others to feel happier, and conversely, if they were cross, did that seem to make others cross? If they were unhappy, what did they do?

Suggested diary headings:

- Thought
- Feeling
- Action
- Outcome
- Date/Time
- What were you thinking?
- How did you feel?
- What did you do?
- Consequences.

Self-control

Self-control enables us to handle our feelings in an appropriate and proportional way so that they facilitate rather than interfere with our task in hand. It is about being able to cope with strong feelings and not be overwhelmed and paralysed by them. This involves:

- managing our emotional reactions: keeping disruptive emotions and impulses in check;

- conscientiousness: taking responsibility for personal performance, controlling our impulses, delaying gratification to pursue goals and recover well from emotional distress;
- being adaptable: showing flexibility in handling change and being comfortable with new ideas, novel approaches and new information.

Once we are aware of our emotions, we can begin to manage our moods and actions. The way we handle our feelings is crucial to developing our Emotional Intelligence. Effective management of emotions implies a prerequisite average or better self-awareness and resolution to use feelings positively.

In a state of low self-control, our actions precede our awareness. We act impulsively. As we develop our sense of self-control, we begin to be aware of rising emotions, prior to acting on them. We can begin to exercise control. Finally, in a state of high self-control, we are aware of what thought has produced the feelings and can use a variety of self-control techniques to guide our behaviour positively. Developing the skills of 'anger management' and 'positive self-image' can enable us to tolerate frustration, avoid put-downs and self-destructive behaviour, and manage loneliness and social anxiety.

What are the skills involved in self-control?
- Managing disruptive emotions and impulses
- Delaying gratification
- Choosing appropriate responses based on understanding the situations or the circumstances we are in
- Self-control and applying appropriate expressions for our emotions
- Expressing anger without fighting: anger management

Managing disruptive emotions and impulses
There are a variety of techniques we can use to control or manage our emotions.
- **Suppressor**: This method involves suppressing our emotions when they occur, controlling or eliminating any outward signs. This technique can be useful in situations where the

display of a particular emotion is inappropriate; for example, we have to suppress our laughter at school assemblies or church services for it could be considered rude, or we might suppress our tears when we do not wish to reveal the magnitude of our disappointment.

- **Reappraisal**: This technique involves mentally changing the situation to produce a more desirable emotional state. For example, a teacher can reassure the learners who are taking an examination that the tests are to inform him/her on how good their teaching has been, and nothing for them to worry about. By controlling the way the situation is defined, reappraisals reduce the level of anxiety we are feeling. Reappraisals allow us to change the personal meaning we attach to a situation, and thus change the emotional consequences of success or failure. Research has consistently found that reappraisals are more popularly used, especially at school.

- **Distracter**: In this method, we handle negative emotions by turning attention away from the distress-producing stimulus and towards something less arousing. For example, involving the children in a singing game they all love when a negative incident occurs distracts them immediately from the need to respond to the negativity.

- **Get help**: In this technique, we respond to the need for emotional control by seeking help from others. When a learner is upset after a playground incident, they might go to the adults to seek help and support.

Delaying gratification

Delaying gratification is the ability to wait in order to obtain something that one wants. This ability is usually considered to be a personality trait. People who lack this trait are said to need instant gratification and may suffer from poor impulse control.

The famous marshmallow test emerged during studies in 1960 by psychologist Walter Mischel and his colleagues at Stanford University, who were examining the ability of children to delay gratification. In a series of experiments, they measured this ability by putting a marshmallow on a plate and telling the child that they could help themselves – or wait until the researcher got back in 15 minutes, in which case they would be given an extra marshmallow.

Predictably enough, about one third of the children gobbled the marshmallow immediately, while the rest decided to wait and get the bigger reward. The researchers were struck by how those who waited devised ways of avoiding temptation, from talking or singing to themselves, to inventing simple games; one even decided to doze off.

The real surprise, however, came a decade later, when Professor Mischel and his colleagues tracked down the children to see what kind of people they were turning into. They found that the children who had been best at delaying gratification had better academic and social skills. They typically achieved much higher Scholastic Aptitude Test scores, were less likely to be distracted, more motivated to succeed and were better at making and keeping friends. They had many of the 'habits of successful people' – confidence, persistence and the capacity to cope with frustration.

On the other hand, the third of the children who had eaten their marshmallow immediately had a very different overall profile. They had trouble subordinating immediate impulses to achieve long-term goals. For example, when it was time to study for the big test, they tended to get distracted into listening to their favourite music or watching TV programmes rather than revising.

The character traits highlighted by the marshmallow test persist in adult life. They affect our performance in every area. Once you start looking for them, it's easy to spot the 'marshmallows' in our professional – and personal – lives. They are the activities which give us immediate gratification but undermine longer-term benefits.

Choosing appropriate responses based on understanding the situations or the circumstances we are in
A famous Greek philosopher, Epictetus, said:

> People are disturbed not only by things, but by the views they take of them.

This demonstrates that self-control can enable us to choose how we see a situation. Should a learner see name-calling, often prevalent in the playground, as abusive and prejudiced to them, or should they see it as a display of poor intelligence and knowledge of true meaning by the caller?

Self-control and applying appropriate expressions for our emotions
Self-control really means being able to control those unproductive behaviours that really don't get us anywhere. We may feel great after a shouting match with a difficult colleague, but the gain is transitory and short-lived. We may have lost a potential friend and done nothing to build effective relationships. Similarly, retaliating angrily in the playground may give a learner the applause of his/her friends but it could only signal bigger troubles with the headteacher and/or parent and feelings of remorse and emptiness when they reflect on their actions.

Expressing anger without fighting: anger management
Anger is a normal human emotion. It can be caused by anything from a friend's annoying behaviour to worries about personal problems or memories of a troubling life event. It generally results from our feeling helpless or unable to control certain situations. We feel as if we are trapped by circumstances and cannot see any way out. Some of us tend to become angry easily ('short-fused') and some of us have problems controlling our anger. Anger has consequences, and they often involve hurting other people – more usually their feelings, but sometimes physically as well. The after-effects of anger often make a person feel guilty and ashamed.

Anger is believed to have three components: the emotion itself, its expression and finally its understanding.

The **emotion itself** is defined as the feeling experienced when our goal is blocked or our needs are frustrated. Examples may include:

- when there is conflict over belonging, e.g. when a child's pencil is snatched away by another child;
- physical contact, e.g. when one child pushes or hits another child;
- verbal conflict, such as a tease or a taunt;
- rejection, e.g. when one child is ignored or not allowed to play with peers;
- issues of compliance, e.g. when children are forced to do something they do not want to do, like wash their hands.

The **expression of anger** could be through facial expressions, crying or sulking, but does little to solve the problem or confront the aggressor. Others could resist by physically or verbally defending their position, self-esteem or possessions in non-aggressive ways. Still others might express anger with aggressive revenge by physically or verbally retaliating against the offender. They might express dislike by telling the offender that he or she cannot play or is not liked. Or they may look for comfort or solution from an adult.

Teachers can provide guidance to help learners express angry feelings in socially constructive ways. Children develop their ideas about how to express their emotions primarily through social interaction within their families, and later by watching television, playing video games or reading books. Some children learn a negative, aggressive approach to expressing anger and, when confronted with everyday anger conflicts, will resort to using aggression in the classroom. A major challenge for teachers is to encourage learners to acknowledge angry feelings, and to help them to express anger in positive and effective ways.

The third component of the anger experience is the **understanding of the anger** – interpreting and evaluating the emotion. Because the ability to regulate the expression of anger is linked to an understanding of the emotion, and because the learner's ability to reflect on their anger is somewhat limited to their age-related cognitive development, they need guidance from parents and teachers in understanding and managing their feelings of anger. Learners may also need several reminders about the less aggressive expressions of anger.

Figure 2.2   An expression of anger

Anger management is the art of learning to express anger in a positive way. It takes as an assumption that anger is a normal and healthy reaction. There are different degrees of anger and each culture will have an appropriate level of anger in a given context. For example, if a child was unfortunate enough to witness their parent being attacked, it would be quite appropriate for them to be very angry and hit the attacker very hard with a stick. The same level of anger and reaction is inappropriate if the offence is at a much lower level, being sworn at in the playground, for instance. The thrust of anger management is to help children in the group readjust their responses in line with the prevailing cultural norms.

The instinctive natural way to express anger is to respond aggressively. Anger is a natural reaction to threats; it allows us to fight and to defend ourselves when we are attacked. We need a certain amount of anger to survive, but on the other hand, we can't physically lash out at every person or object that irritates or annoys us. We can teach learners a variety of ways to deal with their angry feelings:

- We can teach the learners to express their anger assertively rather than aggressively. This may involve stating their needs and/or feelings without hurting each other. They must show respect for themselves and others. For example they might stop, turn around and face the culprit and address them:

'The ball you grabbed from me was my special birthday present and I feel upset that you just took it away without asking me first.'

- Calming down and learning to relax through deep breathing is another useful strategy to share with learners. This could be very helpful in classrooms or any work situation where it is not possible to immediately remove yourself from the situation.
- Change the scene. Sometimes a change of environment can help to reduce angry feelings. For example, if friends are angry frequently and/or make the learner angry, then they must consider moving on and making new friends who might contribute more to their self-confidence and well-being.
- Another technique is to find out the cause of the angry feeling and then find ways of dealing with it. We must learn to

identify what triggered the anger and why. Talking to peers or teachers may help learners to discuss ways of removing that trigger.

Why is it important to control our emotions?

Although it is important to listen to our emotions, it is not always appropriate to vent them immediately, especially when dealing with negative emotions. It may be that the timing is not right, or the setting is inappropriate or the people we are with may not understand us. Our feelings may be excessive, distorted or just inappropriate in relation to the circumstance. They may also have been triggered by feelings that come from a totally unrelated experience.

Self-control is also important in many aspects of our lives. For example, academic achievement suffers when instead of studying for a test, a learner watches TV or joins friends to play; conversely, social relationships are positively enhanced when we talk through a conflict rather than spontaneously retaliate against someone.

The ability to control our emotions also allows us enormous flexibility in our emotional and social lives. Instead of just accepting our emotional state, we can act towards changing it, and making it work for us. We can control arousal levels so as to consistently maximize our performance levels; persist in pursuing our goals despite frustration and temptation; inhibit destructive responses to provocation; and act appropriately despite pressure to do otherwise.

Understanding our own emotions is a prerequisite for self-control and anger management. Therefore, one of the first goals in the classroom is to help learners become aware of what they feel. Once they know what they are feeling, they can begin to see options. Then they can begin to exercise choice. This is the first step in managing our emotions.

It is also important to recognize that we all experience negative emotions like anger, frustration, annoyance, distress and sadness. One way to cope with these difficult feelings is to talk about them, to process them, and to understand that others have these feelings too. This can be very therapeutic, or at least affirming, making us feel less alone and allowing us to move on. It is unwise for our elders or the school to protect young people or staff from difficult emotions. It is empowering to help people recognize and accept the reality and validity of the full range of emotions, which is the first step to managing them well. You cannot manage what you cannot recognize.

How do we develop self-control in the classroom?

- Identify the angry feelings
- Validate feelings through open discussion
- Share strategies for anger management used by the learners
- Investigate novel anger-management strategies
- Investigate triggers for angry emotions
- Model anger management
- Involve parents

Identify the angry feelings (expanding emotional vocabulary)
Teachers can help learners to produce a label for their angry feeling (mad, irritated, angry, cross) which can be displayed as a book or chart. The class can refer to this when discussing angry feelings. Make a class book displaying all the angry emotions of the learners.

Validate feelings through open discussion
Provide opportunities for learners to talk about anger-arousing interactions (situations or people) and discuss constructive ways of dealing with the anger.

Use books and stories about anger to help children understand and manage their own anger. The stories which demonstrate the use of positive and responsible anger-management techniques can help to validate the children's feelings and provide them with alternative ways of dealing with their emotions.

Share strategies for anger management used by the learners
Circle Time starters:

- A time I felt happy/scared
- How I react when I am angry
- I could have hurt someone's feelings, but I didn't
- A time I really controlled my feelings
- A time it was OK to express my feelings.

Give learners the opportunity to describe resiliency behaviours that have helped them get through difficult situations.

Investigate novel anger-management strategies
- Develop the habit of positive self-talk as a way of controlling negative-inducing thoughts and attitudes. Display in the classroom positive affirmations that the learners can use when in difficult situations.
- Learners can be invited to interview someone whose self-control they admire, and report it to the rest of the class.
- Present typical scenarios that involve people in difficult situations, then brainstorm and/or role-play alternative responses and ways of thinking.
- The learners can practise distracting themselves through humour, relaxation exercises or breathing.

Investigate triggers for angry emotions
Are our emotions being triggered by factors 'out there' or 'in here'/within us? Discuss the importance of being aware of what it is about a particular context that may have triggered an emotion.

Encourage children also to look at causes of emotions in others.

Model anger management
Model good self-management skills. When you share your emotions with the pupils, be sure to explain how you are dealing with them. You may also model the recipe for handling strong emotions put together by the class. Acknowledge, accept and take responsibility for your own angry feelings and express your anger in direct and non-aggressive ways.

Involve parents
Communicate to parents the class/school strategies for anger management and enlist their assistance for continuing anger-management procedures at home.

Learners guided towards responsible anger management are more likely to understand and manage angry feelings directly and non-aggressively, and to avoid the stress that often accompanies poor anger management. Teachers can take some of the bumps out of understanding and managing anger by adopting positive guidance strategies.

Empathy

Empathy is the ability to connect with and understand the feelings of others, whether or not we share (or agree with) those feelings. It involves:

- Understanding others: sensing the feelings and perspectives of others and taking an active interest in their concerns, what motivates them, how they work, and how to work cooperatively with them.
- Developing others: sensing the development needs of others and bolstering their abilities.
- Creating and maintaining rapport: people feel safe enough to talk freely to us without the fear of being judged.

To empathize with someone is to understand what they are feeling, or, more precisely, to understand what you would feel like if you were in that situation. Our ability to empathize is directly dependent on our ability of self-awareness. We cannot appreciate other peoples' feelings unless we feel our own. But it is more complex than that; it also requires an awareness that others think of themselves in ways that are both similar to, and different, from the way we do. Empathy may require the subjugation of personal moods or affective states, if the person you are attending to has a greater need.

Empathy is a skill that children learn – it is not dependent on genetics. The best training for empathy begins in infancy, but it is never too late to start. Infants and toddlers learn the most by how their parents treat them when they are cranky, frightened or upset. By the time a child is in preschool, teachers can begin talking to them about how other people feel.

Research indicates that females of all ages exhibit higher levels of empathy than do males. Modelling and training, however, has the potential for reducing the gap between the empathy of boys/men and girls/women.

Similarly, research also demonstrates that adults exhibit a greater degree of empathetic feelings, understanding and responsiveness than children, and older children are more empathetic and pro-social than very young children.

As teachers, we must be aware of these findings and compensate our expectation for age and gender. Modelling empathy is the best way to closing the empathy gap in the classroom.

In a state of low empathy, we are unaware of the feelings of others. Babies and very young children have no concept of others' feelings. As we grow and develop our empathy, we begin to recognize feelings expressed by those around us. In a state of high empathy, we recognize both the expressed and the unexpressed feelings and moods of others.

What are the skills involved in empathy?
- Recognizing feelings in self and others
- Taking the perspective of others
- Listening carefully to others
- Appreciating diversity

Recognizing feelings in self and others
Learners can be taught to be more empathetic by frequently encouraging them to recognize and acknowledge their own feelings. Being aware of their own feelings enables them to undertake the next step of becoming aware of another's feelings – sometimes purely through their tone and body language. The wider the range of emotions that we experiences and the higher our emotional literacy (the ability to correctly identify and label our emotions), the greater are our chances to correctly 'read' another person's emotional message.

Taking the perspective of others
Perspective taking is the capacity to sense another person's thoughts, feelings or behaviour. It is perhaps the most basic and necessary skill in human communication.

Listening carefully to others
Good listening (which includes asking subtle questions, filling in the gaps, and emotionally intelligent guesswork) is essential, as is the ability to interpret non-verbal cues.

Appreciating diversity
Appreciating diversity means accepting others and tolerating differences; understanding that individual and group differences complement one another and add strength and adaptability to the world around us. This enables us to be sensitive and respectful to the feelings of others.

Why is empathy important?
The ability to understand how someone else feels is a vital building block for all social competencies. Empathy allows us to create and maintain a rapport with a broad diversity of people. Learners who can demonstrate empathy tend to do better in school, in social situations, and in their adult careers and relationships.

Cultivating empathy in the classroom can also reduce levels of aggression and violence among learners while raising their Emotional Intelligence.

When learners understand how others feel, they are less likely to victimize them through bullying. As educators, it is necessary to be aware of the social strata of the group of learners in a given class, because this could affect the dynamics in the classroom. An interesting research-study in the United States by Charlene Giannetti and Margaret Sagarese (2001) identified that learners fall into four social categories:

Popular: About 35 per cent of our learners are in this group. This is the 'in' crowd, the athletic child, affluent children and the pretty child. They are the trendsetters. They look like they are in control and having fun.

Fringe: About 10 per cent of the population fall into this category. The fringe group sometimes hangs around with the popular group, but only when invited. This group doesn't know from day to day where they belong. They dress like the popular group and try to act like them as well. For some reason, it is enough for them to be at the beck and call of the popular group.

Friendship Circles: This group comprises about 45 per cent of the population. It consists of small groups of friends. They know they are not popular, but they don't care. They have the friendship and loyalty that they need. These groups may not all be alike.

Loners: This last group consists of about 10 per cent of the population. These children have no friends. There are varied reasons for this. Some of them are very bright, very creative and in a class of their own. Some have very little Emotional Intelligence and use inappropriate behaviour, such as invading personal space. Many of them may wish to be in a group but have never been accepted. Many of these children are unhappy.

Empathy becomes a major factor in the classroom when there are such diverse and obvious social groups. The teacher's role is to raise awareness of how others feel and give opportunities to learners to reflect and identify those feelings in their own experience. Self-awareness here serves as the bridge to really understand the feelings of others. Teacher awareness of the social dynamics of the class and increased empathy among the learners could enhance learning opportunities.

How do we develop empathy in the classroom?
- Focus on learners themselves
- Create a community of learners
- Practise imagining/perceiving another's perspective
- Exposure to emotionally arousing stimuli
- Model empathetic behaviour

Focus on learners themselves
When seeking to increase the ability of learners to assume another's perspective, it is most useful to have them focus first on their own feelings – to identify the different kinds of feelings they have, and analyse/understand what feelings are associated with what kind of situations.

Create a community of learners
- Provide opportunities where learners can take an active interest in each other.
- Provide opportunities for learners to share each other's strengths.

Practise imagining/perceiving another's perspective
Stepping into other people's shoes or using the ability to imagine and gain insight into another person's point of view is for many of

us a hard task to master. Sustained practice at role play or perspective-taking is an effective means of increasing levels of empathy.

Use role play to see what is happening from a different point of view. A popular activity when reading stories is to take the view from another character – for example, we all appreciate the situation of the 'Three Little Pigs' but have we ever stopped to think of the story from the point of the wolf?

In subjects like history, geography or science, try to encourage the learners to take the role of the people in the period of history, geographical areas being studied, or even the scientist or inventor, and imagine how they would feel.

Similarly, encourage or direct learners to study the lives and achievements of famous empathetic people. This increases their desire to be like these people and to take on attitudes and behaviour associated with them. Some examples include Florence Nightingale and Mother Teresa.

A drama strategy called 'Hot Seating' can also encourage learners to develop empathy. One learner volunteers to sit on the 'hot seat' and act the role of a particular character or person, and the rest of the class sit around the hot seat and interview the character being depicted on the chair. The responses given must be in line with the character's thinking and not the learner's own thinking. A class discussion can follow where the learner acting the role explains how easy or difficult it was to assume that role and what empathy or lack of it they had to demonstrate in keeping with the role.

Exposure to emotionally arousing stimuli

Portrayals of misfortune, deprivation or distress in others tend to increase empathetic feelings. Newspaper cuttings, especially photographs of the plight of children around the world, are very effective in developing empathy. Encouragement to think about others and their needs also stimulates these feelings and responses.

Model empathetic behaviour

Teachers who model desired values enhance the learner's empathy. The way adults *show* empathy is more important than anything they say about it. If a three-year-old in the nursery cries out, 'Look at the fat lady!' and you publicly say that s/he shouldn't embarrass other people, you're working against yourself. Instead, quietly and gently explain why saying that may make the woman feel bad. Ask him/her if s/he ever felt bad because of something a person said. Even so, some three-year-olds may be too young to comprehend what you are saying.

At the age of five, however, learners can begin to comprehend empathy by talking about hypothetical problems. How would you feel if someone took a toy away from you? How would your friend feel if someone took a toy away from him? By the time a learner is eight, s/he can grapple with more complex moral decisions in which s/he must realize that someone else's feelings may be different from their own.

Empathy begins with an awareness of another person's feelings. It would be easy if friends and colleagues would tell each other how they feel. But this does not always happen and as individuals we have to be sympathetic, ask questions, read between the lines, watch the body language, guess and try to interpret clues. Once we have figured out how another person feels, we can show empathy by acknowledging their feelings.

In showing empathy we may use empathetic statements. There are appropriate words, phrases or statements that are used to help someone feel better. Some helpful empathetic statements include:

'You sound very upset . . .'
'I can see you are really uncomfortable about this.'
'That must have been difficult for you . . . and . . .'
'It sounds like you've been feeling a lot of pain inside . . .'

In demonstrating empathy, it is important to acknowledge the person's feelings or the situation they are in.

Personal motivation

Personal motivation skills make up the emotional tendencies that guide or facilitate the reaching of goals. These include:

- a drive for achievement: striving to improve or meet a standard of excellence

- commitment: aligning with the goals of the group or organization
- initiative: readiness to act on opportunities
- resilience: persistence in pursuing goals despite obstacles and setbacks.

In a state of low personal motivation, we often feel depressed without an awareness of the cause. People with low self-motivation are inclined to be overwhelmed by affective states, sometimes to the point of paralysis, and rarely 'get the job done'. As we develop our sense of personal motivation, we begin to use self-help talk and focus on goals. Finally, in a state of high personal motivation, we are constantly reframing our thinking and restructuring our tasks. Self-motivated individuals are able to begin a task, stick with it, and move ahead to completion, all the while dealing with any setbacks that may arise. People with high self-motivation are able to focus and concentrate well, and to channel both their cognitive and affective skills into achievement-oriented behaviour.

What are the skills involved in personal motivation?
- Goal orientation
- Achievement drive
- Initiative
- Optimism

Goal orientation
In order for the universe to grant us what we want, we must first decide what we want. This involves marshalling our emotions in order to reach our goals; paying attention – focusing on the task at hand.

Achievement drive
Achievement drive includes striving to improve or meet our personal goals; setting challenging goals and taking calculated risks; and learning how to improve performance. Such drive requires self-control and self-discipline – the ability to delay gratification and stifle impulse. It might also involve a demonstration of commitment and/or resilience.

Initiative

Initiative means being ready to act on opportunities; pursuing goals beyond what is required or expected of us; and actively seeking out opportunities to fulfil the group's mission.

Optimism

Optimism is an outlook on life such that one maintains a view of the world as a positive place. Optimists see the glass as half full, while pessimists see it as half empty. Optimism involves persistence in pursuing our goals despite obstacles and setback.

Why is personal motivation important?

Personal motivation enables us to use our emotions to achieve our goals. Without personal motivation life becomes purely existential. Personal motivation brings meaning to life, and identifies goals to be achieved and heights to be conquered. Every individual must find within themselves something they want to achieve, be or do, and then focus on the task at hand, paying attention, and behaving less impulsively until the task is achieved to the best of their ability.

Research shows that people who have high personal motivation enjoy better psychological health and are able to bounce back after setbacks.

Two decades of research by the United States-based psychologist Csikszentmihalyi show that activities that both challenge and permit us to draw on existing knowledge are most likely to send us into a state of 'flow'.

When thinking about 'using our emotions', try to think of our emotions as a kind of natural resource. In order to achieve certain goals, this resource can be very helpful. Using emotions successfully means being able – when appropriate – to harness the power of this resource in order to reach our goal.

For example, emotions can be employed to improve our ability to persist in the pursuit of a particular aim. Imagine a classroom where behaviour is an issue. The teacher could have a marble jar, and put a marble in the jar for every positive behaviour that is demonstrated by the group. When the jar is full, the group can choose a pleasurable activity to engage in at the end of the day. Whenever the class resolve weakens, the almost full marble jar may deter them from behaving badly and encourage them to persist with their positive behaviour goal. In this case, successfully using emotions would harness the motivating power of engaging in a pleasurable activity.

Another method that teachers can use to encourage positive behaviour is to arrange things so that failure to persist will lead to a highly undesirable outcome. The class could discuss this issue and agree to give away their most sought-after games CD to another class if behaviour is still poor by the end of the week. In this case, the teacher is recruiting the disappointment and unhappiness the class would feel if the prized CD was delivered to the class next door, to bolster the effort to stay calm.

Short-term goals can also be achieved through using emotions in the classroom. A teacher can encourage positive self-talk just before an assessment to steer away the fright and the unrest that precedes these situations.

How can we develop personal motivation in the classroom?
- Goal setting
- Delaying gratification
- Making choices
- Encouraging positive self-belief

Goal setting
Encourage learners to think in terms of meaningful goals for personal development. Discuss what needs to be done to achieve these goals. Work towards their accomplishment. The more meaningful the goal is, the greater the personal motivation to achieve it.

Delaying gratification
Look at the long-term and not the short-term benefits of being able to delay gratification (for example, working hard on an examination now to ensure university entry later). Discuss with learners examples from their own lives. Such discussions will enable the whole class to identify and then work towards own goals.

Making choices
Give learners opportunities to describe situations in which they had to make a choice from two or more undesirable options. Discuss their emotions and behaviours in these situations. Learners may

wish to share the feelings associated with these choices, and possibly the outcomes too.

Encouraging positive self-belief

Encourage and maintain positive emotional states in the classroom as they enlarge the range of thoughts and actions available to the learners. Negative emotional states narrow the focus and constrict the ways one engages with the world. For example, when you are fearful or angry, you are less likely to explore, reach out or be creative; instead you tend to withdraw and look very narrowly at the problem in hand.

Encourage positive self-belief and the use of positive self-talk at all times to broaden the focus and the availability of options at all times.

Relationship skills

Relationship skills refer to the skills for dealing with others in such a way that one is able to get desired results from them and reach personal goals. Such skills are the key to popularity, leadership and interpersonal effectiveness. This would include the ability to:

- communicate: listening openly and sending convincing messages
- influence: employing effective tactics for persuasion
- cooperate: with others and work harmoniously in teams
- manage conflicts: by negotiating and resolving disagreements.

In a state of low relationship skills, we cannot maintain close interpersonal relations with others. As we develop our relationship skills, we begin to maintain friendships but are relatively unskilled in the wider range of social relationships. When we attain high relationship skills, we possess a range of skills including leadership, group facilitation, taskmaster, gatekeeper and friendship skills.

What are the relationship skills?
- Effective communication
- Cooperative learning

- Assertiveness
- Conflict resolution

Effective communication
Communication skills are the key to successful relationships. Effective communication is the ability to use verbal and non-verbal skills to express oneself and promote effective exchanges with others. It involves sending clear and convincing messages for establishing rapport. This means knowing how to join in with what is happening first, before attempting to change a group's behaviour.

The basis of all relationships is communication. It establishes connection, and connection forges a relationship. The adults in the classroom need to be effective models for learners in all the competencies discussed so far, but above all in terms of effective communication. Teachers talk to, and often at, learners, and many of them get little opportunity to experience the thrill of having someone really interested in them and what they have to say. Being listened to constructively adds to one's positive self-concept and a sense of attachment which is essential to learning.

Listening carefully to the learners is also a diagnostic tool for uncovering the vital things teachers need to know about learners – how they learn, what they are learning, what they are having difficulties with and what is coming in the way of their learning.

Cooperative learning
Cooperative learning and paired working enable learners to acquire a set of skills that are absolutely essential for life. The group exerts a pressure in such a way that the following Emotionally Intelligent behaviours are learned:

- How to manage themselves and get along with others
- How to handle their anger (one can't blow up in a group and get away with it)
- How to motivate themselves
- How to persist when the task becomes difficult
- How to resist temptation and stay fixed on a goal and, most importantly
- How to work towards a common goal
- How to know when to take the lead and when to follow, an essential skill for effective cooperation.

Assertiveness

Assertiveness is an attitude and a way of relating to the outside world, backed up by a set of skills for effective communication. To be truly assertive, we need to see ourselves as being of worth and as having a right to enjoy life. At the same time, we value others equally, respecting their right to an opinion and to enjoy themselves. This view allows us to engage respectfully with other people, while also respecting our own needs. Assertiveness ensures that we are not hurt, used or violated. Assertive behaviour is the ability to formulate and communicate our own thoughts and wishes in a clear, direct and non-aggressive way! It is about knowing where we stand, and communicating from that starting point. Assertive statements have three parts: the **facts** – describing the situation; the **feelings** – aroused in us (or the effect the situation has on us); and finally the **want** – asking for a specific action or behaviour agreeable to us. For example, a learner in the classroom may say to his/her friend:

> *'When you took my new pen from my tray, I was worried that I had lost it. Next time, please tell me if you wish to borrow it.'*

Being assertive will raise the learner's self-esteem by showing them how to resist bully tactics and emotional blackmail without using aggression! People who develop good communication skills are able to defuse difficult situations. Assertive behaviour also promotes a positive response in others!

Conflict resolution

A conflict is a fight or struggle; a clashing of opposed principles; or distress due to the opposition of incompatible wishes. Conflict inherently occurs in life at all stages. Therefore, managing conflict constructively and developing conflict resolution procedures is essential for our physical and psychological well-being.

Conflict resolution is about teaching learners new ways to work through and resolve disputes that don't involve violence. Nearly all conflicts involve underlying emotions. The stronger the feelings involved, the more difficult is the resolution. To resolve conflicts, then, it is absolutely necessary to address the feelings of all parties. There are two traditional ways of responding to conflict: fight or flight. Now, there is a third: Solving the problem through dialogue!

In resolving conflicts there is a need to understand the mechanisms at work. People in conflict are generally locked into a self-perpetuating emotional spiral in which the declared subject of conflict is rarely the key issue. Much of the resolution of conflicts calls on using the other emotional skills mentioned here.

The teacher or any trained person can sit with the learners and help them work out their conflict by creating an environment where problem-solving can take place. This is done by strictly enforcing some agreed ground rules: being honest, not interrupting, and no name-calling or put-downs. The teacher-mediator helps the disputants (learners) define their problem, develop solutions and choose a workable solution. Because the disputants are solving the problem themselves, they are invested in the solution. The goal is to have a win-win outcome. (Ask the powerful and positive question: 'What would help you feel better?') This process also helps to get to the root of some persistent problems. However, the process takes time and sometimes the conflict may not be worth the time and effort compared to the learning that comes from it. In many schools, learners are trained to carry out this process by themselves whenever a conflict arises.

Why are relationship skills important?

Since learning is a social activity, relationship skills are critical for dealing with the people we interact with in the classroom. These skills don't come naturally but have to be worked at. They are strongly related to the way we were brought up, our inner feelings about ourselves, our level of confidence and our interest in others. When such skills are missing, it can lead to loneliness, frustration and non-cooperation. Good relationship skills are the invisible glue which binds relationships together. Without these skills we would cause much pain and anguish for our peers and unhappiness for ourselves. Positive relationships provide a gateway for learning.

How can we develop relationship skills in the classroom?

- Provide opportunities for communicating with each other as a group
- Model group roles
- Allow opportunities to develop the skills of assertiveness
- Use problem-based scenarios regularly

Provide opportunities for communicating with each other as a group
- Explore the importance of good listening and discuss how the learners feel when someone refuses to listen to them.
- Talk about ways of getting the attention of another person as a prelude to expressing themselves, and distinguish between positive, effective and negative, ineffective, methods of getting attention.
- Recognize how feelings and moods generated by one incident can be transferred to and affect the outcome of subsequent situations.

Model group roles
When assigning group work, model how to handle the material and respect each participant. Group roles may be a useful strategy to employ in that the members know who is the scribe, narrator, resource collector, etc.

Allow opportunities to develop the skills of assertiveness
The three-pronged statement of Facts, Feelings and Wants needs time to be practised in a friendly environment. It may also be a good idea to practise various hypothetical scenarios where the learners have to formulate the assertive communication. This would then ensure that the learners automatically use such statements when they are faced with overwhelming situations.

Use problem-based scenarios regularly
Short problem-solving sessions with diverse problems will allow the interests and expertise of different group members to emerge, and will show the learners some positive and constructive strategies to engage in when facing a difficult real-life situation.

Summary

Understanding the constituents of Emotional Intelligence enables us to recognize them in ourselves and in those around us. Teachers can support learners to develop the skills they lack through normal classroom routines.

The applications of Emotional Intelligence in the classroom are almost infinite. Emotional Intelligence is instrumental in resolving difficult situations between learners, motivating learners to stay on task until it is completed, and the ability to control impulses and delay gratification. It can motivate learners through goal-setting and dealing appropriately with any setbacks that may arise. It gives them an 'I can do' approach, helps them with understanding other people's point of view, encourages taking responsibility for their own actions, and relating and communicating appropriately with others.

People with high Emotional Intelligence are fun to be with and they are able to:

- express their feelings clearly and directly
- read non-verbal communication
- balance their feelings with reason, logic and reality
- feel empowered
- be intrinsically motivated and emotionally resilient.

Since negative emotions and indirect expression of emotions are all contagious, it is generally smart to avoid people with low Emotional Intelligence. They can infect us with their bitterness bug and victim viruses. These people are not fun to be around with for they:

- don't take responsibility for their feelings
- attack, blame and command you
- interrupt and invalidate you
- carry grudges and withhold information
- have no empathy for others.

Part 3: The ELEVATE Strategies

The challenge for teachers is when and how to teach Emotional Intelligence in their classrooms, given their already crowded day. There are several ways to approach this question.

- Emphasize specific skills, such as conflict-resolution skills, communication skills, relationships or anger management, and teach them separately.
- Incorporate the teaching of skills that are likely to be useful across a wide range of settings and situations. Self-management skills, thinking skills and problem-solving skills are applicable to nearly all domains of life.
- Use teamwork, collaborative learning and small-group discussions to provide opportunities for children to learn to interact with others in a supportive environment.
- Infuse Emotional Intelligence into the teaching and learning of the traditional school subjects by taking advantage of the everyday problems and disputes as they arise in the classroom to help learners develop perspective-taking and conflict-resolution skills.

According to Goleman, however, it is the 'how' that may be more important than 'what' we teach.

> Whether or not there is a class explicitly devoted to Emotional Intelligence may matter far less than how these lessons are taught.

It is this last point, realizing the importance of **how we teach** that goes to the heart of using the seven successful strategies to **ELEVATE** Emotional Intelligence. These strategies illustrate how teachers and learners can put Emotional Intelligence theory into practice. Having introduced and familiarized the class with the concept of Emotional Intelligence, focus on how you teach, and teach in ways that promote Emotional Intelligence. It is not one more thing you have to teach. You can teach the existing curriculum using the seven successful strategies that promote Emotional Intelligence as an embedded curriculum. These strategies structure the interaction of learners with each other, with the curriculum and with the teacher. They are designed to maximize positive educational outcomes. Because the strategies are content-free, they can be used in all year groups and with any curriculum subject.

Knowing about Emotional Intelligence leads to improvement in learners':

- Attitudes (motivation, commitment, understanding of others)
- Behaviour (participation, study habits, impulse control)
- Performance (grades, subject mastery, initiates new learning).

Therefore, instilling emotional and academic learning within your learners is your ultimate achievement as a teacher. So how do you design a classroom that fosters both emotional and intellectual learning? What follows are seven successful strategies – ELEVATE – to be incorporated in the classroom routine, even if your school has not instituted a formal programme in support of Emotional Intelligence.

Environment for learning:	create a safe and positive learning environment
Language of emotions:	build on the language of emotions
Establishing relationships:	caring relationships strengthen learning
Validating feelings:	validating learner's feelings eases tension within
Active engagement:	encourage active engagement
Thinking skills:	integrate higher-order thinking skills into learning
Empower through feedback:	give useful and timely feedback

These seven strategies foster Emotional Intelligence in a number of ways. These are strategies and routines that provide daily instruction in, and opportunity to practise, Emotional Intelligence skills in a meaningful context. These successful strategies are a way of teaching by doing. Rather than lecturing about impulse control, the effective practices allow the learner to practise impulse control on a daily basis. Similarly, learners cannot learn the skills of Emotional Intelligence by hearing lectures about them; they acquire them by repeatedly practising these skills in the supportive environment of the classroom. Use **ELEVATE** to tap into the power of Emotional Intelligence and observe the academic achievement soar!

Environment for learning: create a safe and positive learning environment

The environment in which we learn has far-reaching effects on how well and how much we learn. It is so important that none of the other practices will be effective unless the environment is right. But I want to emphasize that a 'safe' environment refers not only to physical safety; it also includes emotional safety. We do not allow our learners to beat each other up with their fists and therefore we must not allow them to do it with words either.

Why is a safe and positive environment important for learning?

Research has shown that learning occurs more easily in environments free from threat or intimidation. Whenever a learner feels threatened, thoughtful processes give way to survival reactions. Threats to learners can come from the adults or their peers. The adults could humiliate, embarrass, reject and punish learners; all these constitute perceived threats. The behaviour of disruptive peers in an uncontrolled environment, and name-calling, blaming and ridiculing are a further source of threat from the class members. Such behaviours not only prevent the learner from learning but also can impede the learning process for others in the classroom who fear that they will be next.

What does a safe and positive environment look like in a busy classroom?

At the beginning of the academic year, teachers must strive to create a positive and supportive environment in which the learners feel safe, are treated fairly and feel free to express their opinions in class discussions. In such environments learners develop trust in the teacher, exhibit positive behaviours, and sense that learning is encouraged and nurtured. The safe and positive environment can be embedded in the following ways:

- establish a set of class rules
- create a community of learners
- nurture their self-belief through positive affirmations
- have high expectations
- use praise efficiently
- understand the importance of humour.

Establish a set of class rules

It is important to negotiate with the class a set of rules for living and learning in the classroom. The statements must be positive, high-lighting the required actions. This shared process creates a desirable model of cooperative working and helps to give learners a sense of ownership on what goes on in the classroom. Children who have been involved in the decision-making process will find it harder to complain later on about the practices in the classroom. Furthermore, a clear and consistent approach to discipline fosters responsibility and self-control in the learners.

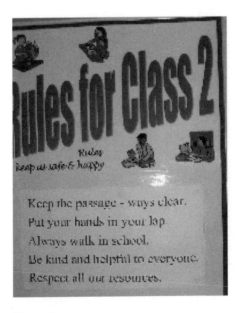

Figure 3.1 Class rules

Create a community of learners

Another strategy is to institute a daily routine that builds a community and creates a positive climate for learning. The adults in the classroom gather together with the learners at the start of the day to greet each other, share personal feelings and accomplishments and preview the planned activities for the day. This helps the learners to settle in; get the burden of feelings off their chest – whether it is the pain of their pet being put down or the joy of a family outing; take a moment to think – rather than react automatically, and often aggressively – to distress and thus be ready to take risks in their learning. When the learners feel safe, comfortable, noticed and confident, they learn. On the other hand, when they are feeling fearful, uncomfortable, ignored or lack confidence, their brains shut down, making learning impossible.

Nurture their self-belief through positive affirmations

Self-belief is an impression (whether accurate or not) that one is capable of performing in a certain manner or attaining certain goals. This belief influences the choices we make and the courses of action we pursue. Learners tend to engage in tasks about which they feel

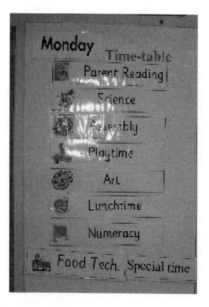

Figure 3.2   Daily timetable

competent and confident and avoid those in which they do not. The higher the sense of self-belief, the greater the effort, persistence and resilience the learner will expend on an activity. As a consequence, positive self-belief exercises are a powerful influence on the level of accomplishment that any learner can ultimately realize.

The teacher's goal in the classroom must be to equip learners not only with the knowledge and the skills, but also the self-belief to be confident and informed citizens – citizens who continue to see themselves as lifelong learners. Positive affirmations should be strategically positioned in the classroom to jog any wavering self-belief. Learners need to be encouraged and reminded to ask each other for help since they understand that everyone in the classroom is a resource. Affirmation posters in the classroom are extremely useful in supporting learning. Our eyes take in an enormous number of messages which get stored in our subconscious mind, to resurface when they are needed. Some messages could include:

'Use what you know to find out what you don't'

*'If you have the courage to begin
You will get the courage to succeed'*

'Success comes in cans not can'ts'

'Each One, Teach One, to show you know'

Figure 3.3 Affirmation

Positive self-belief is one of the most important factors to develop in learners. It is one of the strongest predictors of achievement and enjoyment in school as it challenges their negative thinking and pushes them out of their 'comfort zone'.

Have high expectations

Many researchers have examined the effects that teacher expectations can have on learner's performance; it is suggested that teachers analyse the learners in their class and develop different perceptions of their competencies and potentials. These perceptions are then reflected in the teacher's interaction with the learners, which produces performance in line with the teacher's perceptions, thus fulfilling their prophecy. A study by Robert Rosenthal and Lenore Jacobson in 1968, titled *Pygmalion in the Classroom*, concluded that a learner's intellectual development is largely a response to what teachers expect and how these expectations are communicated to them. The original Pygmalion study involved giving teachers false information about the learning potential of certain learners in Grades One through Six in a San Francisco elementary school. Teachers were told that these learners had been tested and were found to be on the brink of a period of rapid intellectual growth; in reality, the learners had been selected at random. At the end of the experimental period, some of the targeted learners – and particularly those in grades one and two – exhibited performance on IQ tests which was superior to the scores of other learners of similar ability, and superior to what would have been expected of the target learners with no intervention. These results led the researchers to claim that the inflated expectations teachers had for the target learners (and, presumably, the teacher behaviours that accompanied those high expectations) actually caused the learners to experience accelerated intellectual growth.

Teachers, therefore, must have high expectation at all times. They must nurture their learners to learn and achieve by continuously striving for new ways to help them to do so. These actions send messages to the learners that their teacher is there to help them succeed. The young people are therefore empowered to become part of the solution rather than the problem.

Use praise efficiently

Praise is a verbal form of reward for something positive which has been achieved. It is generally accepted that it is an important means of motivating learners. Such encouragement fosters autonomy, positive self-esteem, a willingness to explore, and acceptance of self and others. However, research over the past 30 years has indicated that we need to be careful about how we use praise.

Effective praise is synonymous with encouragement which refers to a positive acknowledgement response that focuses on the learner's efforts or a specific attribute of work completed. Unlike praise generally, effective praise or encouragement does not place a value judgement on the learner's work or give information regarding its value. It focuses on a specific behaviour that the teacher wishes to acknowledge or an improvement and/or effort put into the task in hand. It helps the learners develop an appreciation of their behaviour and achievement. We all have an intrinsic desire to learn. Ineffective praise can stifle the learner's natural curiosity and desire to learn by focusing their attention on extrinsic rewards rather than the intrinsic rewards that come from the task itself.

Teachers should, therefore, use praise so that it is helpful and encouraging rather than harmful and discouraging. Here are some examples:

- Do not praise unimportant or trivial tasks. Praise for an easy task or praise for actions that are below the learner's ability send the message that the learner lacks the ability to do more or better work and that the teacher has low expectation for the learner's success. Unearned or empty praise must be replaced with acknowledgement and suggestions, for example:

'You were able to complete some of today's maths problems correctly, but there are others that you will need to work on.'

- Praise must be specific rather than general. Instead of repeatedly saying:

'Good work!'; or 'Good girl/boy!'

. . . be specific as to what was good about the work or the behaviour, for example,

'You identified the pattern and were able to continue the series.'
'I can read your work because you remembered the finger spaces and the full-stops.'
'Martha has tidied up her table to show us that she has finished her work and is ready for playtime.'

Understand the importance of humour

Humour has many benefits when used frequently and appropriately in the classroom.

Firstly, it has a number of physiological benefits; the brain requires both oxygen and glucose (fuel) to function effectively. When we laugh, more oxygen flows through our bloodstream enhancing the working of the brain. Laughter also causes the release of endorphins in the blood. Endorphins are the body's natural pain-killers, and they cause the person to enjoy the moment in body as well as the mind.

Secondly, humour has psychological and educational benefits; laughter sustains emotional and cognitive engagement, as well as stimulating social presence. It has a role in the learning process since emotions enhance retention by getting the learner's attention and creating a positive climate of bonding together through laughter.

Thirdly, humour can change the way we think about problems and situations. Since teaching is all about transforming a learner's thinking, humour belongs to the teaching tool-kit and should be used frequently. The problem, however, is that the substance of most of what we teach is not very funny. Effective use of humour therefore relies on delivery. Teachers need to develop a mental orientation toward humour, and then exercise it regularly; rather like an athlete who would train for a contest. Some suggestions for introducing humour in the classroom include:

- Use jokes as early morning starter activities – this has the effect of breaking the ice each day; encourage learners to bring in their collection – this would need censoring prior to sharing.
- When mistakes are made, use humour to get through the confusion and difficult content, for example, creating an acronym or a silly sentence to remember tricky spellings, or order of the planets.
- Share stories about failed projects but remember that a great teacher does not have to tell funny stories; they just have to connect truths that will bring out our humorous response.

Finally, humour can also be used as a type of assessment. The time it takes for a 'ping' (i.e. a laugh) to follow a witty comment is a telltale sign about the emotional state of the learners. Our ability to laugh is also a good indicator of the level of tension and energy in the classroom.

How does a safe and positive learning environment foster Emotional Intelligence?

A safe and positive learning environment fosters Emotional Intelligence in many ways:

Self-awareness: The effective use of praise, high expectation and nurturing self-belief at all times enables learners to become familiar with their own strengths and areas for development. They also learn what makes them laugh.

Self-control: Having a set of class rules forces the learners to think about what they say and/or do to their friends; the emotional safety of everyone in the class is honoured and respected. Negative language of any kind is out of bounds and must be transformed into positive statements before they are shared in class.

Personal motivation: The high expectations of the teacher, the effective use of praise, and the nurturing of self-belief all empower the learners, and the fact that they can ask for help from anyone motivates them to have a go rather than give up and sink into helplessness.

Empathy: The community spirit enables the learners to make a special effort to understand and support their peers at all times. Since they also laugh together, it helps to ease the tension and create a bond of understanding between them.

Relationship skills: Learners acquire skills for listening, communicating and supporting each other in their lesson time. They also automatically pick up skills through the modelling of positive skills by the adults in the classroom.

Language of emotions: build on the language of emotions

It is quite hard to discuss our feelings if we have grown up believing that we must hide our true feelings. Therefore, discussing our feelings is an unfamiliar and unknown activity to most of us. As a society, we rarely think about feelings. Every time we feel scared, nervous or even happy we try to cover it up and act 'normal'. We are embarrassed or ashamed, or even afraid, to talk about feelings. It makes us feel vulnerable to discuss feelings publicly. We don't know if we should be honest, or what the consequences might be if we were honest. We are afraid of hurting someone else with our feelings. We might also have been taught that feelings are bad, or weak or too personal to share.

This habit of trying to act different from how we really feel creates many problems in our lives. It creates barriers between us and the people we would like to connect with. Through our inability to reveal ourselves, we also build up stores of resentment, anger and hurt, and end up avoiding people or situations that may cause us to feel uncomfortable. Trying not to show our true feelings to people can often be very stressful. Sometimes, instead of truthfully expressing our feelings clearly and directly, we express the same emotions indirectly, either through our actions or our body language. Sometimes we actually lie about our feelings.

One of the goals of education is therefore to teach learners how to put into words what feelings they have, to themselves and to others, because when those feelings can be put into words, they can be known and they can be managed. Lack of knowledge about feeling words can also lead us to misidentify our emotions. For example, we often see people who are feeling jealous, but we misperceive them as feeling angry. But if we understood what jealousy is as a child, and can identify when we feel jealous, then we can support such people in a way that can help them. Misidentification of feelings is also one of the major issues in relationships. A perfect example is the issue of feeling shy versus conceited. When people are quite shy, they don't initiate conversations and often people perceive them as being conceited, or attribute to them an emotion that is different from shyness, and as a result, treat them differently. So the ability to both recognize and put emotions into words is an important skill for all of us to develop.

A research-study of 300 primary-aged children was conducted in the US in which they were interviewed about their emotions and matched on reading achievement, IQ and behaviour problems as reported by the teachers in their classrooms. What they found was that learners who had more behaviour problems were less able to talk about their emotions.

Why is building on the language of emotions important for learning?

Learning is very much an emotional experience. David Sousa, author of *How the Brain Learns* (2001) emphasizes the emotional dimension of learning but admits, regrettably, that it is the most overlooked aspect. He adds that before learners can turn their attention to cognitive learning or the prescribed curriculum, they must feel physically safe and emotionally secure, and have ample opportunities to share and discuss their feelings. When learners are able to identify their feelings they are better able to take positive action to control them, which in turn makes them better able to work with their peers and get on with the business of learning.

Learning by itself can trigger a range of emotions, because it involves something new and unknown. New learning often includes a risk of failure and discomfort as the learner struggles to make sense of new ideas. Learning can also trigger 'flow', a particular feeling as one engages in the optimum learning experience. Csikszentmihalyi, the Russian researcher on positive psychology, describes 'flow' as a state where the individual is engaged in the pleasure of learning, and learns more than when their learning is forced and the emotional response is fear and anxiety. Hence, flow is based on a balance between perceived safety and challenging learning experiences. The learners' emotional involvement seems to drive their sustained engagement.

How a learner 'feels' about a learning situation also determines the amount of attention they devote to it. Attention is a natural phenomenon guided by interest, novelty, emotion and meaning. Sousa further suggests that emotion interacts with reason to support or inhibit learning. Teachers therefore need to engage learners with such interest and novelty; and that could be why the 'wow' factor and the unique built-in features of the interactive whiteboard in the classroom, for example, enable the learners to concentrate that much more on their learning and decision-making.

What does building on the language of emotions look like in a busy classroom?

Children need to understand their emotions before they can manage them, and they need to understand and manage their own emotions before they can begin to learn new things. Therefore, when it comes to helping children master Emotional Intelligence skills, it all starts with understanding and sharing their emotions. It takes trust and courage to reveal ourselves in the beginning, but it is also true that the more we do it, the easier and more natural it becomes. The following ideas can enable learners to develop a wider language of emotions so that they can express their feelings more succinctly:

- Designate set times or opportunities to talk about the feelings in the classroom
- Create a class list of 'feeling words'
- Use Circle Time routinely to gauge the feelings in the classroom.

Designate set times or opportunities to talk about the feelings in the classroom
Set class times when the learners feel safe to discuss their feelings. The early morning welcome time could be an opportunity for sharing their feelings too. If you spot an unhappy child, approach them gently to discuss their feelings. Ensure validity of their feelings before addressing their behaviour:

> *'It looks like you really don't feel like coming to school today because you're throat is hurting. I understand how you are feeling. Just try to settle in until playtime, we can review the situation then, what do you think?'*

Encourage other adults in the school, such as classroom assistants, parents or students working in class, and midday supervisors, to frequently model the use of the language of emotions to express how they are feeling, how the children are feeling and the general mood in the classroom or the playground. All this will convince the learners that it is OK to talk about feelings and furthermore it will expand their vocabulary of interesting and unusual feeling words they could use.

Create a class list of 'feeling words'
Brainstorm a range of feeling words and display it as a 'feeling wall'. Be creative by being as accurate and precise as possible to extend that list; encourage the learners to look for different words to express the same feelings, and do not forget to emphasize shades of meaning (see Part 2: Self-awareness, pp. 24–9).

Let the class attempt to sort out the range of feelings experienced in different categories. Do the feelings fit in precise categories or can one feeling be in more than one category? Playing with feeling words extends their vocabulary and understanding of these words.

Look at pictures of people and as a class attempt to 'read' their feelings from their faces. Encourage learners to label the feeling rather than the people or the situation. Can they justify their ideas? Such exercises enable learners to be more aware of the body language associated with feelings thus enabling them to recognize feelings in their peers.

Keep a feelings diary for the day/week and let them notice how their feelings change. Can they give explanations as to what caused the changes? Identifying such causes equips us with a list of triggers to be aware of in our lives. Encourage expression of feelings: Label your feeling: I feel ____ at different times in different settings.

In Literacy, always make a point of describing the feelings of the characters in the text. Use the author language to describe the feelings of characters in their creative writing. This is a typical example where reading impacts not only on our understanding of the world but on our speaking and writing too.

Use Circle Time routinely to gauge the feelings in the classroom
Circle Time, created by Jenny Mosley in 1996, is intended to provide an oasis of calm where everyone has equal responsibility and opportunity to speak and listen in a group they can trust. Learners feel comfortable and confident when expressing their feelings, opinions and ideas. Circle Time is underpinned by a number of specific principles:

Everyone in the class sits in a circle. Sitting in a circle gives everyone equal status and an equal voice. There is no hierarchy. Everyone has the right to speak and to be heard. To emphasize this, a 'talking object' is used, such as a small toy – learners may only speak when holding the 'talking object'.

Everyone has a chance to speak. No learner should be interrupted when speaking, emphasizing the need to listen with mutual and growing respect. Learners are not forced to speak; there is no pressure to contribute. If they do not want to comment they simply pass the 'talking object' to the next person. Silence is respected.

It is of great value to teachers to introduce Circle Time into their classroom routine and then use it as a barometer to gauge class feelings. Learners need to be heard and feel heard. The power of Circle Time is its ability to level the playing field. Each learner is given the time to express their thoughts. This prevents strong personalities from dominating and provides an opportunity for shy or hesitant learners to participate. The objective is to create respect and a safe place where all the learners can express themselves authentically.

The ability to wait patiently for the chance to contribute, and to refrain from speaking when someone else is talking takes time to develop, but it is a very important skill which the learners learn quite quickly. They often then remind each other not to interrupt the speaker.

Circle Time allows the learners to identify their emotions and reflect on their behaviour, or ideas and larger concepts, rather than having their responses and thinking overpowered by environmental conditions such as peer pressure or stimulus-response impulses. By listening to others, learners have to make sense of ideas and behaviours different from their own. They can take the time to reason things through. Truly listening to others and respecting their turn to speak helps them to keep quick and thoughtless emotional responses in check. The entire procedure invites learners to put off instant judgement, and trust in the collective answers that emerge.

How does building on the language of emotions foster Emotional Intelligence?

Building on the language of emotions fosters Emotional Intelligence in many ways:

Self-awareness: As learners are given the opportunity to share their emotions in the classroom, they are also encouraged to reflect on their own feelings and understand their triggers, thus becoming more aware of themselves.

Self-control: Having to listen to others talk about their emotions helps learners to hold back their feelings and wait for their turn to speak. Listening to the experience of others sometimes prompts them to delay gratification of their own, so that they stay out of trouble or reap a better reward.

Personal motivation: Recognizing their own emotions frees the learners to set realistic goals for themselves and then, with gentle encouragement from their peers and their teacher, they can successfully achieve their target. Listening to others feelings' and how they cope also enables one to set more challenging targets for themselves.

Empathy: Sharing feelings on a daily basis creates natural empathy within the class. When you know someone is not well or unhappy, you are bound to react sympathetically and empathetically.

Relationship skills: There are ample opportunities to practise communication skills in the daily sharing in the classroom. Listening skills are also developed and improved, as are the problem-solving skills, as we try to guide and support our friends in their learning.

Establishing relationships: caring relationships strengthen learning

In a world of broken relationships and broken promises a strong, supportive relationship is essential in the classroom for learning to take place. We all desire more closeness in our lives. All of us prefer acceptance and approval over rejection and disapproval. The more important the person is to us, the more important their approval and the more intense our fear of their disapproval. Thus, building trust is at the core of success in a teacher/learner relationship. Learners do not generally care how much we know until they know how much we care. Caring relationships between teacher and learner can transform the world of the learners.

Why are caring relationships so important for learning?

Research has shown that positive, caring relationships between teachers and learners can be a determinant factor in the learner's success. Learners care about school, when teachers care about them. The learners who have a warm, genuine and empathetic teacher are engaged in the learning process because they feel that their teacher understands and cares about their needs, and listens and learns from them.

A learner who feels listened to with respect by their teacher and peers feels valued, cared for, appreciated, supported, respected and part of a social group. This empathy motivates them to value, care for, appreciate and feel social towards themselves, their environment, the social group to which they belong, and other people.

Caring relationships also allow teachers to adjust instruction according to each learner's experience and skills. By getting to know learners' personalities, interests, strengths and areas for growth, teachers can provide the right balance of challenge and support. Caring teachers and learners support passionate learning.

What does a caring relationship look like in a busy classroom?

There are a variety of ways by which the teacher can develop caring relationships and strengthen the learning in the classroom. Some of these include:

- Getting to know the learners and developing authentic relationships with them
- Enabling learners to know about each other
- Modelling caring relationships.

Getting to know your learners and developing authentic relationships with them

As simple as it may sound, in order to get to know the learners, it is essential to talk to them. Walking and talking with them, at playtimes, after school and/or at school functions, with no authoritative agenda, creates a set of dynamics that is different from that of the classroom and encourages the learners to talk and divulge their interests, hopes and desires, which you as a teacher can then use as in-roads to captivate and motivate them in the classroom.

Authenticity is being as genuine or as truthful as possible about beliefs and feelings. Being authentic in the classroom means learners and teachers, discuss real issues of concern to them as they occur or become relevant. Issues are not swept under the carpet or ignored. Every member's feelings are considered and discussed appropriately. It is essential that there is an opportunity for learners and teachers to share what is on their mind without fearing ridicule, criticism or judgement.

Teachers must make the time to communicate with each class member and begin to know them as people with whom they can empathise and respect. Many teachers typically greet their learners

with a smile when they enter the classroom and engage them in conversations. They express interest in each learner as an individual and
as a member of the class. Their facial expression and body language
are accepting of the learner' needs, and their vitality and interest
demonstrate involvement, energy and interest in the teaching role.

Enabling learners to know about each other
One idea that could be used is to allocate fifteen minutes every
morning where you enquire about each other. You can call it
'Special Time' because the learners are special people and this is
their time. In secondary schools, this could be done in the form
period when the form tutors meets with their group of learners.
During this session, every class member is given the opportunity to
say what is on their mind. This gives the teacher and the learners
an opportunity to be aware of each others' moods and feelings and
therefore be in a position to understand each others' emotions
and, possibly, to lend a helping hand when required.

Model caring relationships
Learners learn by example, so the way the teachers and other adults
manage their own emotions is always under scrutiny. If the teacher
is unhappy or uninterested in the topic being studied, the learners
will pick up those vibes. When you consider the fact that emotions are contagious even between two strangers, you can begin to
understand the profound effect that the teacher's emotions have
on the learners.

Learners also learn by osmosis. Whether it is apologizing when
we are in the wrong or treating others with respect and kindness,
learners learn a great deal about relationships from observing the
behaviour of their teachers. The adults in the class need to constantly
model the Emotional Intelligence skills, and state the process out
loud. This is a particularly effective strategy for modelling. For
example, the adult might say:

'I am feeling sad about the noise level in the classroom.'

This is an expression of their feelings about a situation in the classroom. It is more effective than shouting about the learners' voices
or screaming at them to be quiet!

Similarly, the adults should be constantly looking out for examples when the children are using their Emotional Intelligence skills, and draw attention to them:

'Mary is sharing her book with Jamie; she knows he is upset about his mummy being in hospital.'

How can caring relationships foster Emotional Intelligence?
Caring Relationships foster Emotional Intelligence in many ways:

Self-awareness: As learners begin to articulate their own opinions to the group, they begin to understand themselves better.

Self-control: Learners have to learn to wait for their turn to make a contribution and cannot just raise their hands and try to win the attention of their teacher. They also have to learn to control their impulse to answer back when comments are made by other members of the class.

Personal motivation: Having positive and caring relationships with their teacher helps learners to set challenging learning goals, which they then accomplish with support from their teacher and/or their peers.

Empathy: Positive relationships, including Circle Time, build cohesiveness within the group and this then encourages empathetic feelings towards each other. Circle Time also provides an opportunity for learners to listen to differing points of view and begin to see the world through another person's viewpoint.

Relationship skills: Listening to others, waiting for your turn to speak, and learning to express yourself clearly are all relationship skills encouraged by Circle Time.

Validating feelings: validating learner's feelings eases the tension within

An awareness of a learner's emotions is the foundation for a healthy relationship. When we are tuned-in to a learner's feelings we are in a much better position to offer support and understanding in our daily interactions. To validate is to acknowledge and accept one's unique identity or individuality. Validation is extremely nurturing; it creates a safety net and builds trust. Validation includes acceptance without passing judgement, empathy, understanding and respect for feelings. Emotional validation is an important skill to be learned in order to have better relationships with people.

Invalidation is to reject, ignore or judge the feelings and/or the identity of others. Sadly, some of us feel the need to put others down and make them feel inadequate, inferior or insignificant. When we are invalidated we are attacked at the deepest level possible, since our feelings are the innermost expression of our individual identity. We invalidate others when we tell them that they should not feel the way they do, tell them they are too sensitive or lead them to believe something is wrong with them. Being aware of the different forms of invalidation helps us to monitor the way various people treat us; be less likely to invalidate others and more able to protect ourselves from its damage.

Why is emotional validation important for learning?

Emotional validation or accepting one's feelings is important because with more validation we will have less debate, less conflict and less disagreement. Painful feelings that are expressed, acknowledged and validated by a trusted listener will diminish. Painful feelings that are ignored will gain strength. For example, when 6 year old Lucy is feeling sad because her best friend has moved away, she might be able to talk about this with her teacher or class-mates. By simply recognizing and expressing her emotions, the chances are that her sadness will not interfere with her learning process. Another example is that when a person is scared, s/he may react with aggression. Validation allows them to interpret accurately the emotional trigger for this behaviour and respond in a manner that addresses the feelings of fear (with reassurance, understanding, etc.).

Providing learners with an outlet to share their experiences, and express their concerns and fears can sometimes make them feel better. The process of expressing or validating these feelings can be helpful for several reasons. Just expressing their fears or concerns can sometimes relieve tension or anxiety in the learner. Sometimes telling and retelling their story can help the learners create a sense of order, coherence or control over events that seem chaotic, confusing or overwhelming, Also, hearing each other's stories may help them realize that they are not alone in their fears or concerns and, finally, the interactions between learner and teacher that come with the sharing of experiences or feelings can build a sense of security and trust.

In fact, if there is a communication breakdown, if there is a wall between you and someone else, it probably has been built with the bricks of invalidation. Validation is the means of chipping away at the wall and opening the free flow of communication. When teachers listen to their learners and show respect for their feelings, opinions and ideas, they provide optimal conditions for attachment and for learning.

How do you validate the feelings of others in a busy classroom?

- First, accept the learner's feelings
- Verbal forms of acceptance
- Non-verbal forms of acceptance

First, accept the learner's feelings

When we validate someone's feelings, we allow them to safely share their feelings and thoughts with us. We reassure them that it is okay to have the feelings they have. We demonstrate that we will still accept them after they have shared their feelings. We let them know that we respect their perception of things at that moment. We help them feel heard, acknowledged, understood and accepted.

Verbal forms of acceptance

The following statements are good examples of validating a learner's feelings:

- *'I know what you mean'*
- *'I would feel the same way'*
- *'I can understand how you feel'*
- *'I can see that you are really upset'*
- *'I can tell this is important to you.'*

After an incident in the playground, validating a learner's feelings with a 'I understand why you felt . . .' is a quick way to diffuse the situation. It also helps us to see things from the point of view of the learner, which helps us to better frame a solution to the problem. Even if a solution is not reached, the learner feels better knowing that someone understands their point of view.

Non-verbal forms of acceptance
Sometimes validation entails listening, sometimes it is a nod or a sign of agreement or understanding, and sometimes it can be a hug or a gentle touch. Sometimes it means being patient when the other person is not ready to talk. Validation is essential to good communication. When someone validates us, we receive what we all yearn for: acceptance, understanding and a sense of connection. This in itself helps us to solve our emotional problems even faster than if we were to be given good advice.

How does validating feelings foster Emotional Intelligence?
Validating feelings foster Emotional Intelligence in many ways:

Self-awareness: To be able to receive validation, learners develop greater self-awareness as they must be able to recognize and express their own feelings before they can communicate them to others.

Self-control: As learners begin to express themselves, they also learn that the listener is not the cause of their tension and therefore they must control themselves as they share negative feelings.

Personal motivation: Validating their feelings sets the learners free to think rationally, set more realistic goals for themselves, and strive hard to achieve them and persevere in the face of setbacks.

Empathy: When learners validate other people's feelings, they show empathy, understanding and acceptance of their feelings.

Relationship skills: The constant sharing of feelings, analysis of situations and emotions helps the learners to think things through, and also trains them to become good listeners. The capacity to listen and to validate another person's feelings improves communication in the classroom, thus building on all the relationship skills.

Active engagement: encourage active engagement

Life is not a spectator sport, it is an exercise in active involvement; and education should thus reflect that activity. In the classroom, we should try to include active, concrete and experiential methods engaging all the senses of the learner. Active learning is generally defined as any instructional method that engages learners in the learning process; it requires learners to do meaningful activities and think about what they are doing. Active learning is often contrasted with the traditional lecture where learners receive information from the teacher.

Active learning implies the development of a community of learners. Essential to this development is communication which involves all learners, in sharing information, questioning, relating ideas, etc. This emphasis on communication provides many situations where learners can produce and manipulate language to support a variety of goals. In other words, active learning supports opportunities for authentic communication rather that rote language drills.

Why is active engagement important for learning?

Active engagement is probably the most overlooked and unappreciated aspect of powerful teaching and learning. It is the key that enables the teacher to move away from providing information to ensuring that learners have many, many opportunities to make personal sense of the material and to learn in real depth. The brain also learns by making connections between what is experienced and what that experience means to the learner. Teachers must invite learners to make connections with what is already organized and stored in the brain. The brain then needs to 'own' the learning; this can be done by inviting the learner to do something with what has been learned. This means that learners must be given opportunities to act in practical ways to answer questions, solve problems and make things happen in relatively realistic contexts.

A teacher cannot assume that a learner has learnt something just because it has been taught. However clear and interesting the material being taught may be, learning will not take place unless the learner attends to it and engages in the mental activity that is needed in order to make sense of the material. The mental activities of the individual learners form a particularly powerful source of influence on what is actually absorbed. This engagement in the activity helps its learning.

Teaching which emphasizes active engagement helps learners process and retain information. To engage the learners, the teacher must help them to draw on their own experiences and build a 'scaffold' on which they can hang new ideas. When learners are actively engaged, they focus on what is being taught and process the new information. A processing act is an act that causes learners to pose questions, manipulate information, and relate the new learning to what they already know. Such engagement reinforces the learning and helps to move it to the long-term memory bank. A processing act can be as simple as a 60-second jotting down of the important points, telling your partner three things that you just learned, or expressing something in a rap.

What does active engagement look like in a busy classroom? The two dimensions of active engagement thus are **independent learning** and **active working** on the part of the learner. Independent learning refers to involving the learner in making decisions about the learning process; active working refers to the extent to which the learner is challenged to use his/her mental abilities while learning. To achieve active learning in the classroom, we need to remember:

- Learning must engage the senses
- Be flexible in the organization of the learning activities
- Role of questions in active engagement
- Role of problem-based learning

Learning must engage the senses
The brain's first contact with the world is through our senses. Therefore learning must engage our senses of sight, hearing, smell, touch and movement. Teachers must provide concrete and physical learning experiences; incorporating language, culture and community resources, not forgetting out-of-school experiences that could be integrated into the instructional activities.

Be flexible in the organization of the learning activities
Teachers must be comfortable to use flexible room arrangements to encourage interaction and sharing of ideas and tasks; and the rules and procedures for working need to be specifically explained to the learners. The role of the teacher may also need to change to a guide and facilitator, rather than a disseminator of information. Learners must also be encouraged to tap into each other's knowledge and experience and build networks for accomplishing goals. Different group strategies – small groups, pairs, individual – must be employed as the situation demands, and the composition of the

groups too must vary depending upon the goals of the activity and the skill levels of the learners.

Role of questions in active engagement
If we want learners to engage actively and deeply in the curriculum, and to engage their whole brain, teachers need to ask different kinds of questions. Questions generate sustained, enriched brain activity. Even after a 'yes' or 'no' question, the brain continues (unconsciously) to process alternatives.

The better the quality of questions, however, the more the brain is challenged and enticed to engage. Interpretive and critical questioning engages the brain more than just factual questioning. Teachers need training and ongoing support to reframe the situation. Learners, too, can be taught to ask one another high-level questions. Benjamin Bloom, an educational psychologist, created the taxonomy for categorizing levels of abstraction of questions that commonly occur in educational settings. This could be very helpful in raising the level of awareness of questioning skills for both teachers and learners.

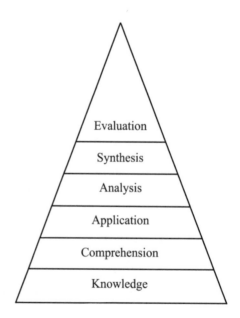

Figure 3.4 Bloom's taxonomy

Bloom divides types of learning into what may be seen as an ascending hierarchy:

- Knowledge (recall of factual information)
- Comprehension (showing understanding of the information recalled)
- Application (consideration of the practical relevance of the information)
- Analysis (the ability to investigate elements of the information)
- Synthesis (using information to move forward in a creative way)
- Evaluation (the ability to make judgements about the nature of information)

Questions can be devised to cover these six areas in the teaching process. This process also allows for differentiation in the formulation of the questions. Broadly speaking, more able learners should be encouraged to explore the higher levels such as analysis, synthesis and evaluation levels. In the planning process, a teacher may consider different types of questions for the different types of learning. Some examples of questions and how it makes learners think are:

'*What do you see in the . . . ?*'
(The learner begins to look more clearly at detail.)

'*Why are you doing this project? What is your goal or learning intention?*'
('The teacher said so', may be true, but it is just an excuse for not thinking.
This question helps the learner begin to see the reason for the project and it could be a major step in making sense of it.)

'*Can you explain it?*'
(A big transition here – for the learner is called upon to talk about and recall the central ideas and concepts.)

'*What would happen if . . . ?*'
(Leaping off to introducing new ideas and possibilities – it forces the learner to spell out their thinking and go beyond obvious answers.)

Role of problem-based learning

A good definition of problem-based learning is that the learning starts from a problem, a question or scenario, within which a number of themes or dimensions of learning are present. In this learning structure the teacher provides the learners with an authentic and relevant problem that is also tied to the current topic being studied. The unit begins with an unstructured, open-ended problem such as the local pond pollution, or recycling or a traffic issue. Learners become involved in the steps of problem-solving: investigative processes, identifying the problem, looking for realistic solutions, considering advantages and disadvantages under the special circumstances, and jointly arriving at a decision. Learners work in groups as they begin their thinking processes regarding possible solutions to the pollution problem. In their teams, they then carry out their particular choice of solution to solve the problem in hand. At the conclusion of the unit, when learners have 'solved' their problem, they again become involved with reflective processing to ensure their deep understanding of the material and to provide opportunities for self-acceptance and team effort.

How can active engagement foster Emotional Intelligence?

Active engagement fosters Emotional Intelligence in many ways:

Self-awareness: As learners get involved in a variety of activities and flexible working arrangements, they become more aware of their strengths and limitations.

Self-control: When they are actively involved in a learning situation, learners have to learn to keep their emotions in check so that they can think clearly through the options available.

Personal motivation: As learners are actively involved in some creative challenge, they are pushed to achieve further so that they can see the end results and achieve satisfaction.

Empathy: Working with others in active settings raises the learner's awareness of their peers' strengths and limitations and enables them to empathize with their feelings and their conditions.

Relationship skills: Invariably learners have to listen, communicate and problem-solve in group situations when actively acquiring new learning.

Thinking skills: integrate higher-order thinking skills into learning

Thinking is the gateway to understanding. It is a deliberate exploration of experience for a purpose. Thinking is using what you know to find out what you don't know. Focusing on thinking skills in the classroom supports cognitive processing, which makes for effective learning. It equips the learner to go beyond the information given, to deal systematically yet flexibly with novel problems and situations, to adopt a critical attitude to information and argument, as well as to communicate effectively.

Higher-order thinking skills are defined as thinking that 'requires learners to manipulate information and ideas in ways that transform their meaning and implications, such as when learners combine facts and ideas in order to synthesize or arrive at some conclusion or interpretation'. This is in contrast with lower-order thinking skills which occur when learners are asked to receive or recite factual information or to employ rules and algorithms through repetitive routines.

Emotions play an important role in the thinking process. If we like what we are learning, we are more likely to maintain interest and move to higher-order thinking. We tend to probe and ask those 'what if' kinds of questions. When we dislike the learning, we usually spend the least amount of time with it and stay at minimal levels of processing.

Why are thinking skills important for learning?

Thinking skills were embedded in the National Curriculum in the belief that they will enhance academic achievement. The essence to a thinking-skills approach to learning is that it increases the learner's ability to notice, understand and work more effectively with what goes on inside their own head. It encourages them to ask questions, solve problems, communicate and work together. Thinking skills thus enable learners to make sense of new information.

Developing thinking skills enhances the learners' speaking, listening, comprehension and writing skills, empowers the learners and builds a community of learners in the classroom who accept each others' points of view and can change their opinion about an issue after a discussion. What research shows consistently is that if you face learners with intellectual challenges and then help them to talk through the problems towards a solution, then you almost literally stretch their minds. They become cleverer, not only in the particular topic, but across the curriculum.

The basic processes of thinking are the same at any age. The older and more able learners may, however, be able to use the processes more skilfully and to weave more knowledge and more subtlety into the use of the processes.

What do thinking skills look like in a busy classroom?

Developing thinking skills requires the adoption of a specific thinking-skills programme and the development of the strategies that extend thinking in the classroom. We will discuss three specific programmes and then elaborate on the strategies to extend thinking.

- Five Thinking Skills in the National Curriculum
- De Bono's Six Thinking Hats
- Philosophy for Children
- Strategies to extend thinking

Whichever programme is selected, we have to teach the programme directly and then allow opportunities to apply it both across the curriculum and in the learners' personal lives as well. When teaching the thinking skill, first introduce the skill, explain what it means and then demonstrate its use. After several demonstrations invite the learners to apply the skill in their learning and then reflect on the skill applied.

It is also extremely helpful when teachers think aloud, or model the use of the skills, in a curriculum area or on a personal issue. An example could be how you decided on what holiday destination to choose, how you responded to a rude teller at the bank, or how you decided to tackle your school workload. Such discussions with the learners assure them that these skills are worth learning because they can be useful to them as adults, and encourage them to adopt the strategies so that they impress others or benefit their own learning and achievement.

Five Thinking Skills in the National Curriculum
Since 1999, thinking skills have been embedded in all subjects in the curriculum. They are placed alongside the other key skills in the National Curriculum, such as those to do with communication and ICT. The five thinking skills include:

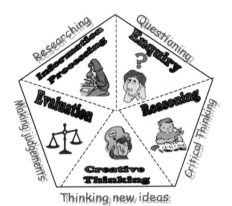

Figure 3.5 Thinking Skills pentagon

Information-processing skills: these enable learners to locate and collect relevant information, to sort, classify, sequence, compare and contrast, and to analyse part/whole relationships.

Enquiry skills: these enable learners to ask relevant questions, to pose and define problems, to plan what to do and how to research, to predict outcomes and to anticipate consequences, and to test conclusions and improve ideas.

Creative-thinking skills: these enable learners to generate and extend ideas, to suggest hypotheses, to use their imagination and to look for alternative innovative outcomes.

Critical-thinking and reasoning skills: these enable learners to give reasons for their opinions and actions, to draw inferences and make deductions, and to use precise language to explain what they think, and to make judgements and decisions informed by reasoning or evidence.

Evaluative skills: enable learners to evaluate information, to judge the value of what they read, hear and do, to develop criteria for judging the value of their own and others' work or ideas, and to have confidence in their judgements.

De Bono's Six Thinking Hats
Edward de Bono is the world's leading authority in the field of direct teaching of thinking skills. He claims that the main difficulty of thinking is confusion. We try to juggle too many balls at once:

feelings, facts, creativity. The six hats allow a thinker to do one thing at a time. Putting on any one of these hats makes us think in a certain way. These six hats therefore provide a simple and practical way to teach thinking as a skill that can be learned, practised and improved. The colour of each hat is related to its function.

- White hat is concerned with objective facts and figures
- Red hat suggests an emotional view
- Black hat points to the weakness in an idea or the negatives effects
- Yellow hat is optimistic and covers positive thinking
- Green hat indicates creativity and new ideas
- Blue hat is concerned with control, the organization of the thinking process and the use of other hats.

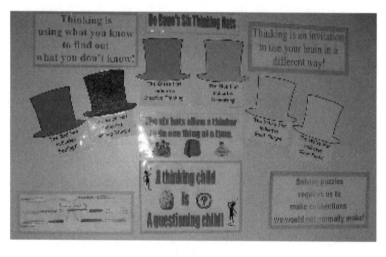

Figure 3.6   De Bono's Six Thinking Hats

Philosophy for Children
Philosophy for Children – widely known through the work of Matthew Lipman, an American professor of philosophy, who developed this method in the 1960s – is a way of encouraging learners to think creatively, logically and reflectively – based on questioning and enquiry. It is a clear-cut process that learners of all abilities can take part in and learn from with some facilitation by their teachers. It is based on the idea that everything is open to

question. The learners are therefore taught how to question and discuss in a way that helps them build on the ideas they have.

What characterizes Philosophy for Children is that learners are not told what they are going to learn about but provoked to ask questions that are relevant to the topic, and to themselves and others. They are then given opportunities to respond thoughtfully to a number of often conflicting arguments and make a judgement based on the evidence presented. They thus become creators of that knowledge which can be applied to a number of other contexts rather than be just passive receptors of information that they will not need or even remember.

A story book is usually used as a stimulus. It is read to the learners and they are invited to ask a question or say what it makes them think or wonder about that story and why. Other starting points that may be used include something the learners have watched on the TV or heard on the news, or even an episode that occurred in the school/classroom /community.

Whatever stimulus is used, learners speedily move into discussions of a philosophical nature and this supports their development of Emotional Intelligence. All the higher-order thinking skills outlined earlier enter into the dialogue and the process makes learners more robust in their thinking and feelings and helps to create empathy with others.

A Philosophy for Children programme strengthens and develops cognitive abilities and Emotional Intelligence. This has been demonstrated by researchers from Dundee University. In 2006 they tracked learners in schools in Clackmannanshire and discovered that Philosophy for Children improved the children's levels of Emotional Intelligence and significantly raised their IQ scores.

Strategies to extend thinking
The following strategies have been found to be successful in helping pupils to extend their thinking in the classroom:
- **Allow thinking time**: after you have asked a question, pause to allow the learners to collect their thoughts and figure out the appropriate response.
- **Think-pair-share**: allow individual thinking time, ask the learners to discuss their ideas with their partners, then share these in a class discussion.

- **Probe or follow up**: probe their understanding further; sample questions include:

'Can you tell us more about that point?'
'What makes you think like that?'
'Do you have any examples or evidence to support your thinking?'
'How do you know that?'
'Does anyone else support that view?'
'Is there an alternative way of thinking or looking at the problem or issue?'

- **Play devil's advocate**: present an alternative point of view and challenge learners to respond by agreeing or disagreeing and explaining their reasoning.
- **Encourage questioning**: discuss what a question is and how it differs from a statement and then invite learners to question a topic being discussed or about an issue that is troubling them. Then make time to allow the group to come up with the answers.
- **Withhold judgement**: by encouraging reasoning and explanations. Sample questions may include: How did you work it out? Or Explain why?
- **Timetable thinking time**: provide opportunities for learners to participate and offer contributions about general issues in class or worldwide.

How can thinking skills foster Emotional Intelligence?

Self-awareness: Discussing lots of issues in the classroom provides the learners with ample opportunities to discover who they really are and what they really believe in, thus enhancing self-awareness.

Self-control: Listening to stories or issues about negative behaviour provides learners with an insight into how they might be perceived if they exhibit such behaviour. This helps them to stay 'in check' so that they are looked upon positively by the group.

Personal motivation: As learners engage in advising their peers or fictitious characters about how best to handle current issues, they are more able to channel their own emotions towards achieving their desired goals. They talk themselves out of quitting when the situation becomes tense and can stand back and guide themselves to persevere until the end.

Empathy: The beauty of reading or listening to stories is that learners develop empathy with the characters as they begin to see the world through their eyes.

Relationship skills: Thinking skills, including Philosophy for Children, develop the learner's communication skills, including the art of listening and problem-solving.

Empower through feedback: give useful and timely feedback

Feedback is information about how we performed in the light of a particular goal; it is value-neutral. It simply describes what we did or did not do in terms of reaching our goals.

Why is feedback important for learning?

Feedback encourages learners and directs change. Jensen (1996) confirms that our brain needs immediate feedback on its own activities for optimal learning and growth. It is therefore important to give feedback regularly in schools as a means to improve learning. There is much research to back up the need for continuous feedback. We cannot learn without feedback. It is not the teaching that causes us to learn, it is the attempts of the learners to perform that cause the learning to happen. This is closely dependent on the quality of the feedback and the opportunities to use it. Feedback that is offered consistently every day feeds the hungry brain's need for reliable correction. All teachers, peers, friends and family members must therefore give periodic feedback for our brain loves feedback because, quite simply, it needs it to survive.

Hands-on learning and the use of technology in the classroom have clearly demonstrated that interactive feedback encourages or motivates learners, and directs their learning. This incremental challenge and immediate feedback in a way that they don't get elsewhere is also what draws youngsters to computer and video games.

How should we give feedback in a busy classroom?

Giving learners grades is now considered to be too little, too late, to be useful feedback. The best feedback is immediate, specific and positive – but almost any is better than none at all.

Feedback can take many forms. The most time-consuming form is individual teacher/learner feedback. This form of feedback clogs up the teacher's time and, therefore, we must encourage other feedback systems from which the teachers can take a step back yet provide the quantity and quality of feedback required for the brain to 'grow'.

First we have to teach the general rules for giving feedback and then explore two very accessible, efficient and surprisingly valuable forms of feedback:

- Pointers for feedback
- Peer-review, and
- Self-assessment.

Pointers for feedback

It is important to keep in mind the following:

- The more often, the better
- The more immediate, the better
- The more specific, the better
- The more appropriately presented to the learner, the better.
- Back up comments with evidence
- Make sure feedback is clearly understood

Some examples include:

'You remembered the full stops. It helped me understand your work better.'
'Wow, Jason, this is your highest test score. I guess that extra practice had an effect.'

Peer-review or assessment

Peer-assessment is the assessment of learners by other learners, a form of innovative assessment which aims to improve the quality of learning and empower learners. It can include learner involvement not only in the final judgements made of other learners' work, but also in criteria-setting prior to learning and the selection of evidence of achievement.

Peer-assessment has many potential benefits to learning for both the learners. It encourages learner autonomy and higher-order thinking skills. Peer-assessment can help self-assessment. By judging the work of others, learners gain insight into their own performance.

Self-assessment

Self-assessment involves learners taking responsibility for monitoring and making judgements about aspects of their own learning. It can be broken down into two stages:

- Identifying standards and/or criteria to apply to an understanding of a subject matter
- Making judgements about the extent to which they have met these criteria.

Self-assessment can be a way of assessing the product of learning but it is a learning process in itself.

Some of the potential advantages of peer- and self-assessment include:

- Providing a sense of ownership of the assessment process and therefore improving motivation
- Encouraging the learners to take responsibility for their own learning
- Treating the assessment process as part of learning, so that errors are learning opportunities rather than failures.

How can giving feedback foster Emotional Intelligence?

Self-awareness: It is only through being open to receiving and understanding feedback that learners can become aware of their strengths and areas of development. Once they are aware of themselves, they can begin to achieve better in class.

Self-control: In the process of peer-assessment, the learners have to manage their own emotions, and control how they feel about the work in order to give feedback that is not judgemental.

Personal motivation: Through self-assessment learners become aware of the task requirements and this motivates them to work towards achieving their target positively. Knowing what is expected of them in order to complete the task also encourages learners to take responsibility for their own learning and persevering in the face of setbacks.

Empathy: Self- and peer-assessment enable learners to develop an understanding of how they feel when given feedback, thus developing empathy towards each other.

Relationship skills: Again, positive communication skills are the crux of self- and peer-assessment; the learners get ample opportunity to develop this and other relationship skills in the process of giving feedback.

Summary

Emotional Intelligence is about us as individuals learning to understand and manage our own emotions more effectively. An Emotionally Intelligent classroom is an environment where emotions are not avoided, but rather elicited in the service of learning. A classroom of Emotionally Intelligent learners should therefore be easy to handle and be a place where much learning takes place. There will be fewer conflicts, and those that arise can be dealt with more constructively.

In such a classroom, the teacher's level of Emotional Intelligence is by far the single most important variable; and the single most important variable in the teacher's Emotional Intelligence is how they handle their own emotions, especially their negative emotions. An effective and successful teacher is largely one who can handle his or her negative feelings in an authentic and positive way.

Teaching about Emotional Intelligence is not a quick fix or a one-off lesson; but using the ELEVATE strategies in the classroom will enable the teacher to gently switch his/her role from spending time with behaviour-management issues to actually having time to spend with the learners and learning.

An Emotionally Intelligent teacher is:
- Infectiously optimistic
- A good listener
- Demonstrates commitment
- Validates other's feelings
- Emotionally resilient.

The role of the teacher in the Emotionally Intelligent classroom is to:
- Spot pressure, keep an eye and intervene when necessary
- Make time for the learners

- Have clear aims and objectives which will be shared with the learners
- Encourage personal development and creativity
- Make time to laugh and have fun with the class.

Finally, learners who experience Emotional Intelligence demonstrate:
- Higher academic motivation and achievement scores
- Better problem-solving and planning skills
- A strong sense of community – make and sustain friendships
- A good understanding of consequences – can resolve conflict fairly
- A positive attitude to school and learning.

Being Emotionally Intelligent is really a dynamic process. It involves give and take, learning and understanding, listening and communicating both thoughts and actions. It enables us to meet our own needs while at the same time meeting the needs of others.

Appendix 1: Emotional Intelligence self-check

The following questions and the quiz below can be used to help learners think about their own Emotional Intelligence.

Emotional Intelligence questions

1. How well do you know your own feelings?
2. Think of a recent problem in school. How were you feeling?
3. How much empathy do you have for others, and how do you express it to them?
4. When was the last time you expressed empathy?
5. Are you sure others are aware of your concern for them?
6. Are you able to understand another's point of view, even during an argument?
7. How do you cope with anger, anxiety and other stressors?
8. Are you able to maintain self-control when stressed?
9. How often do you yell at others?
10. What goals do you have for yourself?
11. What plans do you have for achieving your goals?
12. Do you really listen to others, especially by reflecting back what they are saying?
13. Do you approach social conflict in a thoughtful manner?
14. Do you consider alternatives before deciding on a course of action?

Emotional Intelligence quiz

How would you react in these scenarios?

1. Your friend is rude to you on the phone, and you are feeling a little hurt. You . . .
   - Vow to cut her/him short next time s/he calls you

- Remember that s/he has just lost the main part in the school play and is really stressed out
- Plan something special to cheer her/him
- Call another friend and complain.

2. You hate public speaking. Your new headteacher has just asked you to make a presentation at the next School Council meeting. You . . .
   - Understand that most of your fears are about being unprepared; start researching the topic immediately
   - Make up an excuse that you have a dentist's appointment
   - Agree to do the research but request another student to present.

3. When you are having a rough week in school, you . . .
   - Distract yourself with TV
   - Talk to someone about it
   - Take some time to yourself to explore what is really bothering you

4. You visit your elderly neighbour with some cakes your mum has made. She starts telling you the same story she told you the last time you visited, and the time before. You . . .
   - Tell her that she has told you that story, and ask for another; you know she has a collection of really good stories
   - Nod off; you can't help it after being at the gym
   - Walk out while she is talking.

5. You have been waiting at the bus stop for nearly 20 minutes. The bus finally appears, but keeps on moving, passing you by. It is full of passengers. You . . .
   - Phone your family to tell them you will be late and wait yet again
   - Complain to the other people waiting
   - Shout rude words at the bus driver.

Appendix 2: Who's who in promoting Emotional Intelligence

Epictetus (1st century AD)
A famous Greek philosopher

Publilius Syrus (1st century BC)
Latin writer of maxims

Aristotle (384–322 BC)
One of the most influential of the ancient Greek philosophers

Alfred Binet (1905)
French psychologist working with Théodore Simon who developed the first formal intelligence tests

Edward Thorndike (1920)
Talked about Social Intelligence

David Wechsler (1940)
Psychologist who recognized the importance of 'emotional factors' in our success

R.W.Leeper (1948)
Psychologist who promoted the idea of 'emotional thought'

Benjamin Bloom (1913–99)
An educational psychologist who created the taxonomy of categorizing levels of abstraction of questions used in the classroom

Walter Mischel (1960)
Psychologist who designed the marshmallow test, a test of how 4 year olds managed their emotions (impulse and restraint)

Matthew Lipman (1960)
An American professor of Philosophy, who developed the enquiry method of learning in order to teach learners to think critically, creatively and democratically through philosophical dialogue

Robert Rosenthal and Lenore Jacobson (1968)
Authors of Pygmalion in the Classroom *which studies the relationship between teacher expectation and learners' intellectual development*

Reuvan BarOn (1980)
A pioneer in the field of Emotional Intelligence. He coined EQ as parallel to IQ

Howard Gardner (1983)
Author who wrote about the possibilities of Multiple Intelligence

Edward de Bono (1985)
He is the world's leading authority in the field of direct teaching of thinking as a skill. Author of books on thinking

Jack Mayer and Peter Salovey (1990)
Created the term Emotional Intelligence

M. Csikszentmihalyi (1992)
US-based leading researcher on positive psychology who described 'flow' as being completely absorbed in an activity during which we lose our sense of time and have feelings of great satisfaction

Daniel Goleman (1995)
Author, who popularized the concept through his bestseller Emotional Intelligence

Jenny Mosley (1998)
Author of Quality Circle Time in the Classroom

Eric Jensen (1998)
Member of the Society of Neuroscience and author of brain-based learning books

Charlene Giannetti and Margaret Sagarese (2001)
Conducted a US-based study of cliques in schools and identified four categories to which all learners fall: Popular, Fringe, Friendship groups and Loners

David Sousa (2001)
Author of How the Brain Learns

Useful organizations

- Antidote (www.antidote.org.uk)

A UK organization campaigning for Emotional Literacy. Antidote was set up by a group of people, from diverse professional backgrounds, who saw a need to apply the latest understandings of human nature to the challenge of creating a healthier and more sustainable, prosperous society. Antidote's focus was on emotional literacy, which came to be defined as:

> *the practice of interacting in ways that build understanding of our own and others' emotions, then using this understanding to shape our actions.*

- NELIG (www.nelig.com)

The National Emotional Literacy Interest Group was established in 2000 by Peter Sharp at Southampton Psychology Service. It is dedicated to the promotion of Emotional Literacy for everyone, adults and children alike.

- Sapere (www.sapere.org.uk)

Sapere is an educational charity whose members are interested in the role of philosophical enquiry in education. It was set up in 1992 to build on the work of Matthew Lipman and promote approaches to developing better reasoning and more reflection in schools.

- School of Emotional Literacy (www.schoolofemotional-literacy. com)

The School of Emotional Literacy was established in 1996 to bring materials to assess Emotional Literacy in Europe.

Further reading

Csikszentmihalyi, M. (1992), *Flow: the classic work on how to achieve happiness*. London: Harper & Row.

de Bono, Edward (1985), *Six Thinking Hats*. London: Penguin.

Gardner, H. (1983), *Frames of Mind*. New York: Basic Books.

Giannetti, C. and Sagarese, M. (2001), *Cliques*. New York: Broadway Books.

Goleman, D. (1996), *Emotional Intelligence*. London: Bloomsbury.

Jensen, E. (1996), *Completing the Puzzle: The Brain-compatible Approach to Learning*. Del Mar CA: The Brain Store Inc.

Mayer, J. and Salovey, P. (1997), 'What is Emotional Intelligence?' in P. Salovey and S. Shulter (eds), *Emotional Intelligence and Emotional Development*. New York: Basic Books.

Mosley, J. (1996), *Quality Circle Time in the Classroom*. Wisbech: LDA.

Rosenthal, R. and Jacobson, L. (1968), *Pygmalion in the Classroom*. New York: Holt, Reinhart & Winston.

Sousa, D. (2001), *How the Brain Learns* (2nd edn). Thousand Oaks, CA: Corwin Press.

Index